TRUE BLUE

A PARLIAMENT STREET PUBLICATION

EDITED BY ELIZABETH ANDERSON AND DAVID BEAN

Contents

A note from the editors 3

Reigniting Conservatism 4

Aspiration, excellence and opportunity: the case for grammar schools 6

Preventing demand on policing from cases involving mental health 17

Home Ownership for All : Non-Statist Solutions for the Housing Crisis 26

'A New Form of Politics': Brexit, Immigration and the rise of Populism in Europe 43

The Brexit effect on the City: short term pain for long term economic gain 61

Me, Myself and AI 68

Reviving Conservatism in the Capital 72

The Future of the Conservative Party 78

A note from the editors

True Blue is the second book released by Parliament Street, and the first associated with new Policy Centre Tory Democracy. Parliament Street itself is apolitical, bring together politically aware individuals from all points on the political spectrum, right and left wing.

In line with the position taken by Parliament Street, where there is no corporate view taken by the organisation, each of our essayists and writers is free to express their own opinion. As such, the contents of this book should be taken as the opinion and research of the relevant writer(s), rather than that of Parliament Street or of the editors.

We hope you enjoy reading this compilation. To find out more about the work of Parliament Street, visit www.parliamentstreet.org

Reigniting Conservatism

-- by Clare George-Hilley, Head of Research for Parliament Street; former London Borough Councillor and Chairman of South Richmond Conservatives

I am delighted to introduce Parliament Street's latest book, 'True Blue'. This book compiles a collection of essays from leading Conservatives, academics and business leaders.

Each chapter provides thought-provoking policy ideas and recommendations for the Conservative Party to adopt in the coming months and years.

These are testing times for the Conservative Party, as we struggle to assert our ideas and principles since losing our overall majority.

Since the Conservative Party installed a Prime Minister into Downing Street in 2010, it has slowly buried Conservatism and failed to stand up for its core values. This has allowed the opposition to tarnish us as selfish, greedy and mean. If we do not stand up for Conservatism and win the battle of ideas, I believe that we will lose power completely.

The Conservative Party needs to explain why tax cuts can help businesses create jobs and spread prosperity which is fundamental for a flourishing fair and equal society.

We need to shout loudly about the merits of Conservatism and how over the past decade our policies have transformed education and welfare to help the disadvantaged.

Under the leadership of Conservative stalwarts Iain Duncan-Smith and Michael Gove overall poverty has significantly reduced, unemployment has dramatically fallen and many hundreds of failing schools have surpassed their private school counterparts resulting in 86% of children now attending a Good or Outstanding OFSTED ranked school.

However, we never clearly communicate these Conservative success stories to voters. Instead, we choose to ignore them and try to imitate Labour policies, alienating our core support and weakening the Conservative brand.

This approach had catastrophic consequences in the 2017 General Election, leaving our party wounded and our members deeply disillusioned with the current leadership and direction of the party. Indeed, why should people vote for us if we cannot bring ourselves to outline how a society delivers growth and aspiration through low taxation, individual freedom and healthy competition?

I believe the time has come to set out a positive vision for the future of the country and defend our strong record in Government. We have improved the life prospects for millions of people, unshackling low earners from paying income tax which was raised from £6,500 to £11,500, encouraging hundreds of thousands of people off welfare and into work.

Nowhere is our record stronger than in job creation with the current employment rate at 74.9% - the highest since records began. The UK economy is now the fast growing of all G7 countries and we have a bright future ahead.

Ultimately we need to explain why capitalism is the fairest system of governance and show how every citizen has and will flourish under Conservative principles and values. That's how we will win the hearts and minds of voters and a full majority at the next election.

Aspiration, excellence and opportunity: the case for grammar schools

-- by Elizabeth Anderson, Head of Membership for Parliament Street; Co-Chair Tory Democracy, and Conservative activist and former council candidate

Last year, when new Prime Minister Theresa May first stated a firm intention to look at lifting the ban on grammar schools, educationalists and politicians immediately split into two.

Some were pleased that the government was taking a progressive stand that might help to raise the life chances and academic aspirations of children and young people across the country, building on educational reform to boost social mobility amongst the next generation. Others believed that the creation of new grammar schools was a backwards step that could damage equality.

One could argue that the root of the question on grammar schools is really whether we should encourage and celebrate excellence over equality. But there is also the important question of ensuring that we provide educational opportunities that allow **all** children to fulfil their full potential, whether or not that is academic.

Background

Grammar schools date back centuries, but the Education Act 1944 formalised their role in the education system as the focus of academic learning, with those who failed the 11+ examination expected to instead attend their secondary modern. The expectation of the day was that those who attended the latter would take a less skilled career path.

They were gradually phased out and replaced with comprehensive schools, which instead aimed to give a more rounded education, with successive Labour governments suggesting that this would break down class divides. The School Standards and Framework Act 1998 – brought in by the new Labour government – outlawed the creation of new grammar schools, although existing schools survived in some areas such as Kent and Buckinghamshire.

In 2016, the new Prime Minister, Theresa May, announced a consultation into lifting the ban. With grammar schools keen to expand and to create satellite sites, and with parental demand to increase grammar school places and make the system available across the country, the Conservative government felt it timely to revisit the debate nearly twenty years after the ban. This caused debate on both sides, which is addressed through this paper.

A ladder to social mobility

One of the principal arguments that opponents of grammar schools level at the type of education is that it will create a two tier education system that leads to disadvantage.

However, growing numbers of parents already pay for their children to access private education. The Independent Schools Council found that 517,000 pupils enrolled in 2015, the greatest number in their 40 year history of records[1]. They choose these selective forms of education because they believe that such schools offer the best life chances for their sons and daughters. Private schools often give focus to core academic subjects which can – for the right people – offer the chance to enter affluent professions. They help children and young people build capacity, confidence and networks that will serve them well as they move to university and beyond into the workplace. And so bringing back state funded grammar school education allows children and young people from any background to access an academic education that otherwise could be outside their reach. This is an essential element of social mobility – in a world in which the biggest foreteller of a child's future remains the level of qualification possessed by their parents. Shortly after the announcement of the proposal to lift the ban, over a third of parents surveyed by YouGov[2] felt that grammar schools would actively increase social mobility, with only 19% thinking that it could cause any damage.

We add to this that grammar schools already exist. A report by the Centre for Social Justice found nationally that just 3% of the attendees of grammar schools were eligible for free school meals – the key barometer of low income students. One reason for this is the small number of such schools,

---

[1] https://www.theguardian.com/education/2015/may/01/private-schools-in-uk-attracting-record-numbers-of-students
[2] https://yougov.co.uk/news/2016/08/15/two-thirds-people-would-send-their-child-grammar-s/

another is the location of the schools – which are commonly located in the more affluent areas of the home counties. Even without grammar schools in the equation, many parents who can afford to choose to move to an area with a 'good school' to give their child the best chance of an education to set them up for life. A Centre for Social Justice report[3] cited research by Lloyds Bank that:

> "...house prices in the postal districts of the top 30 state schools in England – defined as those secondary schools that achieved the best GCSE results in 2015 – were on average £53,426 (17%) higher than the neighbouring locations in their county. The postal districts of six of the 30 top state schools commanded a house price premium of over £150,000 compared to their surrounding locations."

The result of this is an education system that favours those whose parents have higher incomes. By opening state funded grammar schools across the country, we enable young people to attain more highly based on their own aptitude, aspirations and motivation, rather than the earning potential of their parents.

Whilst the Sutton Trust has stated considerable reservations regarding the accessibility of grammar schools to those from poorer backgrounds, they stated in their 2008 paper "Social selectivity of state schools and the impact of grammars"[4] that research shows that "*pupils who attend grammar schools do better than equally able pupils in comprehensives.*"

However, separately, the Sutton Trust also found that "*95% of the top 500 comprehensives take fewer pupils on free school meals than the total proportion in their local areas, including almost two thirds (64%) which are unrepresentative of their local authority area with gaps of five or more percentage points.*" This does little to evidence that grammar schools are any less likely to support children from low income families than comprehensive schools.

---

[3] http://www.centreforsocialjustice.org.uk/core/wp-content/uploads/2016/12/161201-Grammar-School-Report.pdf
[4] http://www.suttontrust.com/wp-content/uploads/2008/10/GrammarsReviewSummary.pdf

And, the Sutton Trust's reservations, highlighted in their report *Poor Grammar*[5] also highlight that disadvantaged children may not gain a grammar school education through lack of confidence from adults. Reasons given by head teachers in the report include that parents may feel that grammar school is elitist, or if attending a primary school filled with high achievers, that their child is not good enough. By opening up the grammar school system again, placing them all over the country, and re-normalising grammar school education, these unfounded concerns could be massively reduced.

Their report also suggested that tests be more frequently refreshed, and created in such a way that would minimise the ability for more affluent parents to arrange 'coaching' for their children which might skew the results of entrance examinations. The 11+ need not be incompatible with the range of educational institutions which have been created through the recent education reforms, particularly those driven through by Michael Gove. But the test must be fair to all, and not designed to favour those who can afford exam practice and tuition solely to pass the exam. Such a means of testing does not provide a firm foundation for testing the true talent and mindset of a child, and it is essential that feedback from headteachers is utilised, and replicate the type of education children might receive in primary school – such as creative writing and numerical skills. Equally, it is important that primary schools provide the support that children need to prepare to pass the examination if they do indeed have the ability to do so.

According to Daily Mail columnist Peter Hitchens[6], "a 2006 Freedom of Information request to Oxford and Cambridge universities found that fewer than 20 per cent of state secondaries provided all the state-school entrants to Oxbridge. Most of them came from grammar schools." Within the same article, Hitchens states in the by-gone days of a national grammar school system, 64% of their students came from the working class. This strongly suggests that a determining factor for grammar school education was not class or wealth, but pure aptitude.

And it cannot be right that academically minded and gifted children are held back by an education system that currently fails them by providing a 'one size fits all' system which holds them back. Conversely, those from wealthier

---

[5] http://www.suttontrust.com/researcharchive/poor-grammar-entry-grammar-schools-disadvantaged-pupils-england/

families are more able to access an academic education – either by attending private schools, or with parents ever more willing to pay for private tuition.

Even at an anecdotal level, those who have attended both types of school but with an academic leaning have found that grammar schools are more supportive. In a blog for Conservative Workers and Trade Unionists[7], Richard Short states:

> *"The grammar school is where academically minded pupils can excel in academic subjects, be proud about it and not, as I was in both the comprehensives I attended, bullied for it. As a grammar school pupil you are much more likely to be with others who want to learn in a similar way. Like it or not the comprehensive system fails those pupils who want to excel at academic subjects. At comprehensive school the pool of talent is so broad and the desires for children to learn so varied and inconsistent it is difficult to give children of different abilities the differing attention they need to either excel or to get on at all."*

And Chris Philp MP, a leading backbench proponent of grammar schools has also talked about his experience of state-funded grammar school education, and the benefits to him as an 'ordinary' child[8]:

> *"What grammar schools do is give children from ordinary backgrounds the chance to achieve their potential. It's something I've got experience of - I was offered a place at Trinity in Croydon but even with a scholarship my parents couldn't afford to pay the fees so I went to a grammar school next door in Bromley. Without that grammar school I wouldn't have got to Oxford and I certainly wouldn't be Croydon South's member of Parliament."*

The English education system is seeing ever greater demand for more schools – more have to be opened in order to provide every child with the education which is their right. But there is no fairness in forcing children with very different abilities and interests to learn together.

---

[6] http://www.dailymail.co.uk/debate/article-4415470/PETER-HITCHENS-sleek-elite-hate-grammars.html#ixzz4egWlogDM
[7] http://www.toryworkers.co.uk/grammarschoolssocialjustice/
[8] http://www.croydonguardian.co.uk/news/13875730.Boost_for_plans_to_open_Croydon_s_first_grammar_school_in_decades/

University Technical Colleges already exist, in small numbers, to allow those with a strong interest in a practical subject – such as marine engineering or media technology – to focus their studies on subjects and applied learning relevant to that interest from the age of 14. There can be no reason not to allow a similar focus on more academic subjects, given an appropriate method of selection.

The introduction of greater choice also means that children – with the support of their parents – are able to start considering their strengths at an earlier age. Whilst no primary school child can realistically know what career they are likely to want, they will have a sense for the subjects they enjoy. Their teachers will be able to deduce where their strengths lie. The current school system expects children to work hard across the board, with no choices taken until GCSE options.

This, in some ways, is what the original Academies programme was looking to achieve under the Labour government. The first Academies were required to choose a specialism – from sports to mathematics to business and many others – and even to select up to 10% of their cohort based on aptitude for some subjects[9]. Additional funding was received based on the school's performance with that specialism. When the requirement to specialise was removed by Michael Gove in order to reduce bureaucratic burden, so much of the focus of specialist schools fell away (although this does not mean they no longer exist, with some schools and Academies continuing to maintain one or more specialisms). But this is a recent precedent for children choosing to attend a school that could cater to their specific interests.

The consultation which was launched last year, with a response due in spring 2017, also looked at how to ensure that grammar schools would go beyond their 'normal' cohort as perceived by some parents. This included ensuring that catchments areas were wide enough to be not prohibitively expensive, and that grammar schools might be forced to sponsor a non-selective academy or free school, potentially including feeder primaries that would be accessible to all.

---

[9] https://www.theguardian.com/education/2007/may/22/schools.uk3

Growing demand

It is also worth considering that there is a great demand for grammar school places. According to the House of Commons Library[10], there are currently 163 grammar schools in England with a total of 167,000 pupils. According to the Sutton Trust[11], there were 161,000 students in 2013. Take-up is increasing, and that is without new schools opening.

In 2016, YouGov published detailed research on the demand for grammar school places, as a result of Theresa May's announcement of the consultation on lifting the ban. They polled over 80,000 adults across England. Their findings[12] showed resounding support for grammar school places.

> "...nearly six in ten people (62%) would get their child to sit the entrance exam for a grammar school if there was one locally, whilst two thirds (67%) would send their child to a grammar school if they passed the exam."

This snapshot shows that parents would like the option, and two thirds would seek for their child to take up the opportunity given the chance. Tellingly, there was support for the creation of new grammar schools even from those parents who had not attended on themselves – and had therefore failed the 11+. The research[13] shows that 61% of those who attended grammar school thought more should be created, and that even a third of those who had been at a secondary modern thought the creation of more grammar schools was a good idea.

In London, most boroughs are firmly in favour of the creation of more grammar schools – the most pro-grammar school area in the country is in south London – and parents are keen to see policy ideas turned into practice. Chris Philp - Conservative MP for Croydon South who is

---

[10] http://researchbriefings.parliament.uk/ResearchBriefing/Summary/SN01398#fullreport
[11] http://www.suttontrust.com/newsarchive/sutton-trust-prep-schools-provide-four-times-grammar-school-entrants-fsm-pupils/
[12] https://yougov.co.uk/news/2016/09/09/new-map-shows-where-new-grammar-schools-would-be-m/
[13] https://yougov.co.uk/news/2016/08/15/two-thirds-people-would-send-their-child-grammar-s/

campaigning for a grammar school in the London Borough of Croydon states[14]:

> "The demand from parents for grammar school places is extremely high and far outstrips supply – for example, Sutton's grammar schools have 10 applicants for every available place; 30 per cent of these schools' pupils come from Croydon."

Grammar schools in Kent are looking at means of expansion and the creation of satellite sites, which could, in the short term, help to meet demand. But in the long term, more grammar schools are needed to keep up with parental demand.

Supporting those with different aspirations

Another of the accusations levelled at grammar schools is that they create stigma for those who fail to make the grade to get into them – or indeed have no interest in following the types of career path opened up by grammar school. It is only right, as well, that there is a broad range of opportunities – the country needs an equally broad range of skills which cannot all be achieved if everyone takes the same path.

It is not right to hold back children who could achieve academic greatness because it might cause offence to others. The UK jobs marketplace is crying out for those with STEM skills – science, technology, engineering and mathematics. Many of these skills require the academic focus and aptitude that grammar schools are so well equipped to provide.

These academic learning hubs allow stretching educational targets to be set and met. Teachers who choose to work at the establishments want to succeed in their own careers and are motivated to provide encouragement and inspirational learning to their students. Classwork is not set to the 'lowest common denominator' as can be the case in classes in some less well achieving schools. Distractions can be less for students because of the type of students who have achieved to get into the school. Like any school, this still requires strong pastoral care, including ensuring that children are not over-pressurised, and that values such as team-working and community interest are developed.

---

[14]

http://www.croydonguardian.co.uk/news/13875730.Boost_for_plans_to_open_Croydon_s_first_grammar_school_in_decades/

However, it is equally important that we do not return to a system that sees children who are not academically gifted being sidelined. A child who fails an exam should not be allowed to spiral into a self-fulfilling prophecy that prevents them from ever achieving at anything – ditto a child who chooses not to follow an academic path or does not have the aptitude. This simply means that their skills lie in a different direction, and it is important that reforms that lead to the creation of grammar schools do not leave these children behind. Through Academies, free schools, UTCs, Studio Schools and general educational policy, we need a diverse education system that provides a range of opportunities and route maps for children to build the skills that they need. This could range of practical and applied learning in engineering, to computer programming, to manual skills and sporting prowess.

There also remains a wider stigma that needs to be dispelled. Apprenticeships are currently undergoing a very long term rebrand – one that has been ongoing for well over a decade. There are similarities between the role of university over an apprenticeship with that of grammar school over comprehensive. Neither educational route is necessarily 'better' than another – but for every child one (or another option) will be more suitable, more fulfilling and more useful for their chosen career path.

Not every child wants or can be a top scientist, business leader or academic – with the coming of Brexit, we need to be supporting the next generation to develop skills of every type and level, and grammar schools are just one very important part of the educational reforms we need to support this. And we would not even consider banning academic university education (which is by its very nature selective) because it might make those undertaking an apprenticeship feel less worthy.

Improvement across the board

The UK lags behind a range of far eastern and European countries in league tables. The Programme for International Student Assessment (PISA) tables for 2015, published by the Organisation for Economic Co-operation and Development (OECD) in December 2016, show that in the key subjects of science, reading and mathematics, the UK's schools need to up their game –

with students scoring especially poorly in maths, and standards declining. According to the Daily Telegraph's[15] analysis of the data:

> "some 22 per cent of 15-year-olds in the UK do not reach Level 2 - the baseline level of achievement - which means they cannot solve problems "routinely faced by adults in their daily lives".

The result of this could be that the country continues to look overseas for talent, at the expense of providing our own children with the skills they need to access skilled and professional employment – thereby barring our own young people from accessing employment.

In England and Wales there are areas with outstanding schools in affluent areas. There are also pockets of incredible deprivation, which can often see children in schools which require improvement – although there are examples of very highly achieving schools or individuals within these areas. But there is, without a doubt, inequality of education already. There are many reasons for this, which are outside the scope of this paper. But we do not live in a world in which every child in this country has an equal chance of an outstanding education. Moreover, more affluent parents are able to pay for their child to access the type of education that a grammar school can provide, further widening the attainment gap, and, if anything doing more to reduce educational equality of opportunity.

Grammar schools introduce competition into the educational marketplace. This is competitiveness of school offer – not competition between children. In grammar school selection, it is for the child to demonstrate an academic aptitude to a certain bar in order to gain an offer. This is not in itself dissimilar from university entry, where one needs a certain level of points to get into the university of choice on the course of choice.

This means three things:

- Parents with any aspiration for their child want their child to do well. They therefore support learning. Whether this support leads to academic excellence or excellence in other fields is beside the point – encouraging parents to engage in and support their children's

---

[15] http://www.telegraph.co.uk/education/2016/12/06/oecd-pisa-report-does-uk-rank-international-school-league-tables/

education can create the type of environment that allows a child to focus on their school career.
- Primary schools who want to attract children and parents have to step up to the plate to offer the education that will support children to make it into the local grammar school. Of course, it remains important that non-academic children are not sidelined, and maintain the support and type of education that they need to excel in other areas.
- Secondary schools who don't want to be left behind or see poor attainment also have to step up to make an offer to young people and their parents. In the 21st century, no school head wants to run a 'sink school' to rival the bad old days. This is absolutely key. This means that schools offering other types of education – from sports academies to University Technical Colleges to comprehensives must raise their own game to ensure that they offer an alternative that parents and students alike can be proud to attend.

Conclusion

Grammar school education provides an excellent foundation for academically minded students, and it is recognised by experts that children achieve better outcomes when they attend such a school. Given this, and that parental demand for grammar school places remains high across the country, it makes sense that the government presses on with its intentions to lift the ban.

At the same time, it is very important that other educational opportunities remain in place and continue to build on their own excellence. The UK has a fantastic opportunity to create the next and future generations of children who have the skills we need – helping to create families who can support themselves and drive our economy forward. We also need to ensure that primary education prepares children for whatever route they and their parents want to take – and giving them the skills that they need to face whatever type of selection style the grammar schools of the near future might adopt.

By adding grammar schools to a growing range of educational establishments, we can give parents and children further choice in their education, and diversify the type of skills that our children can acquire in their formative years. And such choice can only be good.

Preventing demand on policing from cases involving mental health
-- by Matthew Scott, Police and Crime Commissioner for Kent

Summary:

- The demand on Policing as a result of cases involving mental health continues to rise, with some Forces reporting that demand takes up to 57% of their time in some parts of the country

- However, in some areas, Police Forces don't know the full picture or fully understand the demand on their time

- The cost of searching for missing persons where mental health is known to be a contributing factor is around £200 million per year, the same as investigating burglary

- Police Forces have made good progress in reducing the number of people detained under section 136 of the Mental Health Act, and fewer are ending up in Police cells

- Police and Crime Commissioners, as elected representatives, can and are raising awareness and enabling public debate on this key challenge by funding projects and holding all agencies to account

- More progress needs to be made in preventing demand, not just managing it

Proposals:

- Police Forces need to undertake detailed work to understand what demand looks like in their own areas

- Wellbeing cafes could be set up in all parts of the country where they don't exist to provide people support and help them manage their own mental health

- Consideration needs to be given to expanding telephone services, such as 111, to include mental health more distinctly
- Information sharing between agencies could be improved so that we can be more proactive, but in a way that is safe and fair
- The ban on the use of Police cells for detaining young people under section 136 of the Mental Health Act needs to be implemented, and a similar ban brought in for adult detentions too
- Substance misuse service providers could look at their substance misuse and addiction services to see if alternative places of safety can be provided when someone has been detained by Police due to concerns about their mental health when they are intoxicated

Police and Crime Commissioners are elected by the public to set Policing priorities, be a voice for victims and commission support for them, work on community safety schemes with partner agencies and hold their Force to account for service delivery. We set the budget and the council tax precept and have a role to play in the complaints process. Due to our political roles, we also have the ability and freedom to raise concerns with and make complaints to other organisations that Chief Officers may not be able to do.
This paper is an example of how Police and Crime Commissioners are not just holding our own Police Forces to account on behalf of taxpayers, but how we are making representations when extra demand is being placed on Officers and Staff from cases involving mental health and standing up for people in need, above and beyond the valuable work done by Mental Health Crisis Care Concordats.

Parliament Street's campaigning to raise awareness of mental health and the impact it is having on policing is welcome, and I am pleased to have written for their report recently on this matter. I strongly believe that the challenges faced by Police Forces across the country by the demand placed on them by cases involving mental health is one of the biggest that needs to be addressed. This is not to say that British Policing UK is responsible for the solution – they absolutely are not. However, we need new ideas, programmes and investment in mental health so that Police Forces are not either picking up the pieces for other statutory agencies or placed in difficult situations by a lack of care prior to the individual's interaction with the Police.

The principle must be, as I have put in my own Police and Crime Plan, that people suffering from mental ill health need the right care from the right person at the right time. In too many cases locally and nationally, this is not what is happening despite more Police and Crime Commissioners making it a priority.

The demand on Policing

In my area, in Kent, the Police spend around one third of their time dealing with cases involving mental health. In Medway, the figure is 57% and in Thanet it is 50%. This is not sustainable in the long term, not the right attention that people suffering from crisis need and not fair on the individual Officers who have to attend the calls received.

Most of the attention with regards to mental health and policing has been focused on detentions under section 136 of the Mental Health Act. It gives Police Officers the power to detain someone who is in a public place and they feel that they need immediate care or control. They need to check with a health professional first and they can either keep them where they are or move them on so that they can get a mental health assessment.

In the last twelve months, the use of section 136 by Kent Police Officers rose by around 240 to 1333, but due to improved care pathways, there has been a dramatic drop off in the number ending up in a Police cell in the last six months. Due to various schemes nationally, Police cell use has fallen and some Forces report a drop in section 136 detentions. But this is just the tip of the iceberg.

The National Crime Agency recently published data that showed that Police Forces dealt with 335,624 missing persons reports in 2015/6. This means that a report was made every 90 seconds. The data showed that 21% of the people who went missing suffered from a mental health condition, depression or anxiety. To put this into a financial context: the Centre for the Study of Missing Persons (CSMP) at the University of Portsmouth estimated that a missing persons investigation costs Police Forces between £1325 and £2415 each time, based on a Force spending 14% of all its time looking for missing people. I have not included dementia in this estimate or commentary, which is specified as a reason in another 3% of cases where people go missing.

Dr Karen Greene, from the Centre, estimated that the annual cost to Policing nationally of missing persons investigations could be as high as £800million. Using the figure of 21% of missing persons cases having an element of mental health as a contributing factor, it could be argued that this aspect alone is costing Police Forces well over £200 million per year – the same as it costs to investigate burglary. The more we can do to help people manage their mental health, understand the reasons why people go missing and provide earlier intervention, can prevent demand to Policing that sadly often occurs.

Missing persons and crisis are just two examples of demand that the Police face from cases involving mental health. There are many more, from those victims who are being exploited by organised crime gangs to commit crime on their behalf or give them the premises to do so, to fraud and sexual exploitation, or even just instances where they meet people whilst on patrol. Demand is rising and this is acknowledged by Policing and NHS bodies.

Managing demand

There are many schemes now that have been set up to help Forces manage the demand that they experience. One of the most popular is street triage, where Police Officers and mental health professionals go out to calls together. In parts of the country this has shown some statistical success. Policing areas that have this scheme have seen a reduction in the number of people detained under section 136 of the Mental Health Act by Officers, and thankfully, a reduction in the number subsequently held in a Police cell whilst they wait for a proper health-based assessment to take place.

The reason why I include this scheme under the heading of "managing demand" rather than "preventing demand" is that whilst some Officer time is potentially being saved and custody facilities freed up, there is still a cost to Police Forces for providing the Officer(s) to drive the mental health professionals to the calls. So whilst the person is getting support from a mental health professional, which is what we want, it still comes at a cost to Policing.

In Kent, we have another scheme that helps manage demand. I have commissioned counsellors from MIND to work in the Force Control Room, where 101 and 999 calls come into the Police. Nationally it is estimated that 6% of all calls to the Police involve mental health. In one month, Kent Police will answer 75,000 calls to 999 or 101, which means we can estimate that 4500 calls will involve an element of mental health in some way every month.

At specific times of the week, these trained counsellors can take on calls from handlers where a mental health issue has been identified and it is safe for that person to be dealt with in this way. This helps to free up call handlers and does, on occasion, mean that the individual contacting Kent Police gets better advice than they would have done otherwise and Officers are not dispatched. Their presence also means that call handlers and Officers can also ask for advice on cases.

The scheme has recently been extended so that they are looking to do more proactive work and outreach, potentially with those who are known to Kent Police and contact them frequently. This would be to see which agencies can better support them, where appropriate.

However, this is not always possible, as there are various standards of information sharing between agencies in different parts of the country. Essex, for example, has a very good working relationship between agencies to share data within the county but others do not. Another issue is that Essex would not be allowed to share their information with Kent Police so easily. This problem needs to be addressed in a fair and proportionate way.

Many other Forces have similar telephone-based schemes, but recent plans implemented in Cambridgeshire are taking a different approach. If you ring 111, the NHS Direct number, you will be given an "Option 2", which will be to talk about your mental health. I was greatly heartened by this as this is a good example of NHS bodies working together to prevent, not just manage demand and challenges the mindset that the Police should be the response to mental ill health, not the NHS. I would like to see this rolled out further if the model proves to be successful.

Intoxication

Intoxication is another issue that can cause real difficulties for Policing. For example, if someone is intoxicated, then they cannot be assessed if they have been detained under section 136 of the Mental Health Act. This adds to further pressures and stresses between the NHS and Police when there is no capacity or any place for them to wait until they can be looked at.

To put this problem in context, it has been suggested to me by clinical commissioners from other parts of the UK that intoxication is a factor in between 20% to 50% of section 136 detentions. So we do need to ask public health commissioners if they can look at their drug and alcohol services and see what more can be done to link better with mental health services and provide a place of safety for those who are being detained and intoxicated. This would provide a safe place for the individual, potentially act as an intervention and help manage demand on police resources such as custody.

Here you have an outline assessment of what we have at the moment, and a proposal for another scheme to help manage demand from the appropriate provider. Programmes that help Police Forces to manage demand are welcome, but sometimes require the investment of the Police and Crime Commissioner and Chief Constable in order to get them off the ground or to ensure their continued presence.

What we also need to see more of are schemes that fall into a "preventing demand" category, as Police contact is too late and options for earlier intervention may have been missed.

Alternative places of safety and earlier intervention

The previous Government had already started work in this area. Last Summer, they ran an Alternative Health-Based Places of Safety capital funding campaign that allowed local Mental Health Crisis Care Concordat groups to bid for a share of £15million to provide some of these earlier interventions. Much of the funding focused on improving hospital settings or section 136 suites and the pathways, but Kent was successful in receiving a small proportion of this money for outreach and community support.

I was recently invited to open one of the successful projects that received funding from the Department of Health in Kent. MIND in Tonbridge received £9000 in order to upgrade their facilities in order to provide a wellbeing café for people who wanted a safe space to talk about their own mental health and perhaps support others too. Money has also been provided by West Kent Clinical Commissioning Group and me in order to pay for professionals to run the café and provide guidance on managing conditions and referring people into the services that they need. They are open presently for eight hours a week, in the evenings, and dovetail with another scheme that both the CCG and I fund, so that from Thursday to Sunday, in West Kent, there is an alternative place of safety available for someone to access.

The outcomes from the first month have been positive. 48 people have attended and feedback has been sought. If the facility had not been there, one in three would have contacted the mental health crisis team for help, and one in four would have gone to accident and emergency instead. Whilst we cannot draw any long term conclusions from one month of data, similar schemes elsewhere do show similar benefits. The impact though cannot just be measured in statistics or funding – behind every number is an individual. The Solace café received feedback from one person that said "Attending the

Hope and Solace Café has helped to save my life". I think that speaks volumes.

"Crisis" or "wellbeing" cafes are not a new concept. In fact, there have been some running in Kent and other parts of the county for several years. In 2014, the Safe Haven Café opened in Aldershot. As an alternative to visiting accident and emergency. It provides out of hours care and advice to people who want it and is staffed by both NHS workers and third sector partners. It had a dramatic impact on their A&E attendance numbers of a drop of around one third. The feedback from users shows that it has helped to prevent suicides, and helped people deal with loneliness, homelessness and general crisis.

Using a model of out of hours support via a wellbeing cafe could provide one of the solutions to preventing demand, if the NHS and others can work together to commission more of them. For example, if a charity could be loaned an appropriate premises by a council, GP surgery or private enterprise, for a few hours week, or use their own if possible, a scheme like this could get off the ground in every area quickly and cheaply. You could in theory have one such alternative place of safety in each council area in England for an amount in the tens of millions, rather than hundreds of millions of pounds, providing much needed service when other avenues aren't available.

There are two challenges that I am aware of to these schemes. The first is making sure that the right organisation is picking up the bill for the costs of providing these services, so that it does not always fall to the Police and Crime Commissioner or the Police to pay for reducing the demand caused by a lack of other services. The second is that by making it easier to access these types of services that you in turn do not create a dependency, but you empower people to support themselves and one another to manage their mental health in the longer-term. Many wellbeing programmes look to develop peer support programmes as part of their offer, and this is welcome.

The night time economy

There are also examples of where schemes run during the night in town centres can support better mental health and wellbeing. In Maidstone, the Urban Blue Bus, funded by the Council, sponsorship and myself, has two functions. By day, it travels the area raising awareness of educational / awareness programs on health, substance abuse, sexual health, self harm, suicide, race / hate crime, drug and alcohol abuse, fire and rescue and road safety. On a Saturday night, it is an alternative place of safety and treatment for people in the night time economy, providing first aid, a place to wait and counselling on emotional and substance misuse issues. This helps reduce demand on the NHS and on Policing because the demand is prevented, not just managed.

Similar schemes run in other parts of the country too and have shown some success in reducing pressure on the emergency services. Buses like this are a great asset, and I am supporting not just Maidstone's but Medway's. We must also remember the positive work being done by Street Pastors too, who provide this service on their patrols in town centres. They give out advice, directions and basic equipment to help people stay safe on a night out and prevent injury, and someone to talk to. I know that in my area, some of these groups are looking to expand their capabilities by undertaking mental health first aid training, which would be of real benefit to people they meet in an evening, whether they be revellers or homeless.

Conclusions

Policing has always had an element of responsibility for dealing with cases involving mental health and they will continue to do so. This will never and should not change as we are talking about people in need, not just rules, finances and statistics. However, there has to be a fundamental shift away from just managing the high demand we have to real schemes to help prevent demand in the first place. We need to see greater awareness of the support that is on offer and not simply a mindset that says the response to a crisis or mental health call should always be by the Police, not the NHS. That's why I believe the Cambridgeshire model, using NHS Direct, should be considered by all areas as a means of reducing call demand on Policing services.

Statutory bodies should be providing alternative places of safety such as wellbeing cafes, investment in resilience and helping people manage their own mental health so that we can provide the earlier intervention that is needed to help prevent mental health demand falling to the Police. The proposed ban on the use of Police cells for children detained under section 136 needs to be pursued by the new Government. The proposed limitations on their use for adult detentions extended to ban this practice as well, a plan which I know that Chief Constables are voluntarily working towards. More needs to be done to enable better data sharing, so more proactive work can be done to support those in frequent contact with the Police to get them the care they need.

The benefit to Policing is clear. For every demand reduction of 1%, Kent taxpayers get back at least £2.5million of Policing time, or around 50 PCs. That's what I am working towards and my colleagues are looking at too in each of our counties and will be a big factor in increasing Police visibility. When the election is over, I will be lobbying the next Government to see if some of these changes can be made, as I believe that these proposals I believe could go along way to delivering a demand reduction but also ensuring that people suffering from mental ill health get the right care from the right person at the right time.

Home Ownership for All : Non-Statist Solutions for the Housing Crisis
-- by JP Floru, Westminster City Councillor

80% of Brits aspire to own their own home; but fewer and fewer realise their dream. So it comes as no surprise that politicians are increasingly consumed by this subject. The party which makes home ownership possible for the many, is likely to be in power for a very, very long time.

It is now nah impossible for under 35-year olds to buy their own home. Just twenty years ago the prospect was real. Most bought their home, and have been riding the property value dragon ever higher. It is certainly not true that house buying was *easy* in the past: then, as now, most had to save and be parsimonious before and after moving in. But it was certainly *easier*, especially for two income households. You were typically able to borrow 95% of up to three times you annual salary.

Today, the ease to buy is a distant memory; and the dream ever to own property has died for many. What happened?

For most of the second part of the 20th century the number of people owning their own home went up. In 1918, 77% of households in England and Wales rented. From 1953 onwards, home ownership started to rise. By 1971 there was an equal percentage of households owning and renting. Margaret Thatcher kept winning elections on the promise of a 'property owning democracy.' Private home ownership peaked in 2003, when 71 % of the English households owned their own home.

After 2003, private home ownership started to fall. In financial year 2015-16, it stood at 62.9 %. During the same period private home ownership increased in Europe:

England	71 % (2003)	62.9 % (2015)[16]
France	56.1 % (2002)	57.7 % (2015)[17]
Germany[18]	42.2 (2002)[19]	51.9 (2015)

Today in the UK, the decline in home ownership among young people is even starker than for the population as a whole. In 2001, 2 million 25 to 34-year-olds owned their own home; a decade later it was 1.3 million[20]. An entire generation of young adults in the UK have been dubbed 'generation rent': stuck in house shares or with their parents until their thirties, with little chance of ever being able to call a patch their own. They have to commute from far distances to go into work. Over the same period, more and more people came to own their property outright, without mortgage. In other words: fewer own property, but those who do are wealthier.

The nature of tenancies has changed over the years. The number of private renters has increased, but the number of social renters declined. This is partly because many social tenants bought their family homes under Margaret Thatcher's 'Right to Buy' - scheme. Between 1980 and 2013, almost 1.9 million houses were bought by the social tenants who lived there.

Britain's addiction to social housing

Britain has one of the highest percentages of social housing in the Western World. Yet demand for it is again rising. One has to wonder when enough is

---

[16] Home ownership in England falls to 30-year low, by Judith Evans, Financial Times, 2 March 2017
[17] What percentage of French people own property and rent property?, English Speaking Real Estate Agents France, May 2016.
[18] In 1996, Chancellor Kohl's government of centre-right Christian Democrat Party and the classical liberal Free Democrats introduced the *Eigenheimzulage* (the 'Own Home Subsidy'). Instead of subsidising social rents, they would subsidise home ownership. It was believed private home ownership would improve fiscal, urban, and social policy. With a more liberal planning policy than in the UK, the free market kept up with demand and produced more houses.
[19] Home Ownership - Getting In, Getting From, Getting Out, by J. Doling, IOS Press, 2006.
[20] Britain falls behind most of Europe for home ownership, by John Bingham, The Daily Telegraph, 31 October 2016.

enough. Is it normal in a dynamic and prosperous society to subsidise 4 million households in perpetuity[21]?

At the beginning of the 20th century, about 10% of housing was owner occupied; the rest was privately rented. A number of social policies made it increasingly unattractive to rent out homes privately, and private rentals declined up to the 1980s. Public social housing increased steadily, from 1% in 1918, to 31% in 1981. The private rental market picked up again with the introduction of the Assured Short-hold Tenancy, which allowed landlords to recover their property more easily if their tenants defaulted.

Today, 18.6 % of the housing stock in Great Britain are socially rented from local authorities or social landlords such as housing associations. Compare this to France, with 16% of social housing; and Germany with 5 %. In the EU, only Denmark, Austria, and the Netherlands have a higher percentage of social housing than Great Britain[22]. In London the percentage of social housing is even higher: 24%. Social house building differs from year to year, but generally it has remained stable over the last decade or so, with between 40,000 and 60,000 homes finished in any one year.

Another anomaly is that most social houses are granted for life; and that some are even passed on to the children. 200,000 families live in houses granted before Richard Nixon was President. It does not take into account changed financial circumstances. It is the same as saying that one is entitled to child benefit in old age, because one was young, once. Social tenancies for life have only been abolished since 2015, when the government introduced fixed term tenancies.

The Social Housing Spiral

As house prices and rents rise, fewer people can afford to buy or rent a property on the open private market. So more and more people get onto the waiting list for social housing. There are more than 1.8 million households waiting for a social home - an increase of 81% since 1997[23].

The longer and longer waiting lists have led to an increased demand from housing charities, social housing builders, and politicians, for more social house building.

---

[21] Don't dither, Margaret, by Lee Rowley, ConservativeHome, 17 November 2008.
[22] Social housing in Europe, by Scanlon, Arrigoitia, and Whitehead, 2015.
[23] Shelter

Perversely, increasing social housebuilding will lead to even longer waiting lists. The UK's rigid planning system rations the availability of building land: it limits supply. In any given year, part of that will be built upon with private housing, and part of it with social housing. If the social housing ratio increases, then there will be less private house building.

Fewer private properties to buy, means ever higher private property prices. This is exacerbated in mixed developments, where the private housing share is made to pay for the social housing share.

So even more will apply to be put on the social housing list. It is a spiral: the more social housing you build, the more demand there will be. More social housebuilding means that proportionally, fewer and fewer people will own their own home.

Does social housing increase votes for Labour?

Are social housing tenants ardent Labour Party voters? It is said that the then Leader of London County Council, Herbert Morrison (grandfather of Peter Mandelson), wanted to 'build the Tories out of London' - by targeted council estate building to influence local voting patterns.

A study of the 1997 Blair election victory shows that in the decades before 1997, statistics persistently confirmed that a large majority of social tenants vote Labour; that a majority of private home owners vote Conservatives; and that those renting privately do not really express a Conservative or Labour voting pattern either way[24].

A study of the election of 2015 showed that of all the social characteristics such as gender, age, social class, age, and ethnicity, whether one is a social housing tenant gives the greatest likelihood of voting Labour. This is only beaten by BME status[25].

The evidence is clear: the more social houses, the more votes will go to the socialists. Perhaps this is why the Labour Party always opposed the opportunity for social housing tenants to buy their own home.

But there is more to it. When you build insufficient numbers of houses in general, some who fall short, i.e. are unable to buy a house or have to pay

---

[24] Voting and the housing market, by Dorling, Pattie, and Johnston, Council of Mortgage Lenders, 1999.
[25] IPSOS MORI : How Britain voted in 2015

excessive rents, will start to resent the system. Most may not be aware of the reasons behind the lack in house building (such as: rationing because our planning system is too rigid). They end up blaming 'the system', i.e. 'capitalism.' In the 1950s, a West German politician observed that across Western Europe, the share of votes going to communist parties was inversely related to the number of houses built[26].

Why is home ownership declining?

Home ownership has become unaffordable because of house price inflation. UK house prices and rents are among the highest in the world; both in absolute terms, and relative to average incomes.

Since 1970, average house prices have risen four and a half fold after inflation. No other OECD country has even come close. In most English regions you now need five times the median annual income to buy a median house. In the south of England it is 6 times. Grenfell Tower, the social housing block which was consumed by fire, was located in the Royal Borough of Kensington and Chelsea...where the average house price is 38 times average earnings. In most developed countries the ratio is between 2 and 3. Until the 1990s, this was also true in the UK.

House price rises are followed by rent increases. Those in the bottom quintile of the income distribution often spend 40% of their income on housing. The high costs reduces mobility to move to better jobs - as the better jobs tend to be where the housing shortage is the most acute.

In the last two decades people have become rich simply by sitting on their property. Often the property value increase is higher than the owner's employment income. As the shortage of housing becomes more acute, those renting have to pay ever larger chunks of their income to property owners. Those aspiring to buy need to obtain every higher mortgages and put in ever higher deposits.

The unusual increase in property prices has led to a transfer of wealth from those who don't own, to those who own. If home ownership continues to decline in the UK, there will be an electoral backlash against home owners.

Which factors exacerbate house price inflation?

---

[26]How the housing crisis has created a generation of socialists, by Kristian Niemietz, CapX, 2017

A large number of factors are blamed for house price inflation: immigration, atomisation of households, interest rates, tax, the greenbelt, and now even Brexit. But one other factor - the most important one - is rarely, if ever, mentioned by politicians and housing action groups.

Immigration

In a speech in December 2012, Theresa May said that more than a third of all new housing demand in Britain was caused by immigration. She continued: "There is evidence that without the demand caused by mass immigration, house prices could be 10% lower over a 20-year period."

In 2016/17, the House of Lords Select Committee on Economic Affairs concluded that 300,000 new homes are needed annually to cope with demand. Net migration to England alone is expected to be in the region of 233,000 a year (it has been much higher in some years), requiring 240,000 new homes for each year of the next 25 years.

It seems pretty obvious that with such numbers of net migration, demand for housing, and therefore house prices, rise. And yet, one should not blame migration in itself. Migration has not caused a shortage of shops or restaurants or car repair shops. It has only caused a shortage in the housing market, where government regulation has made if difficult for the market to cater adequately for the demand.

Atomisation of households

More and more people postpone or do not enter into marriage or cohabitation at all. Add to this the high divorce levels, and people living longer (often on their own) - and suddenly we need far more houses.

Greenbelts

Greenbelts are another reason for rising housing costs. The vociferous defence of the greenbelt and assorted campaigns to thwart house building on greenfields are not just the result of a conservative 'let's change nothing at all' - attitude. Part of the population believe that the UK is already 'concreted over'. In fact, nothing could be further from the truth: only 1/10 of England is 'developed'; and even that area mostly consists of gardens. Literally 'concreted over' land only covers 1/20 of England. Large parts of continental Europe have a far greater population density than England.

While most want to preserve the environment, simply drawing a circle around cities and forbidding all development there seems a bit silly. In the age of factory farming, many fields are not exactly bucolic havens[27]. We could easily exempt verdant land (woods and meadows) from new development. Blanket development bans are not helpful and amount to rationing of land.

In view of the housing shortage, there are not many options apart from building on greenfields and some greenbelt. In London, almost all brownfield sites already have house building plans. Even at trivial densities, developing just 4 % of London's greenbelt could provide one million houses.

Interest rates

Somebody who rents a flat, pays for a consumption good. Somebody who owns a flat, will not only enjoy the consumption good (if he lives in it), but also have money stacked into an asset that will usually) increase in value over time.

A person with capital at his disposal has many alternatives to obtain the highest return. So if national interest rates go up (bank interest, bonds), he may invest his capital therein (he can e.g. rent in the meantime). If interest rates go down, he will seek other alternatives. E.g. shares, or property. Since the banking crisis, government has kept interest rates artificially low in this country. And presto: equities go up, and house prices rise faster than rental yields.

Brexit?

House price inflation in the UK has slowed down or even slightly declined in the last year or so (2016-2017). The decrease of house prices was caused by both an increase in stamp duty (see below), but also by a reduction in demand. In Central London, a large percentage of properties used to be bought by overseas investors, and by EU citizens who live and work in the UK. Before Brexit, when a nice flat went up for sale in Central London, typically half or more of those who came to view it, were foreigners. Both the foreign investors and the EU buyers have largely stayed away since the Brexit vote.

The dramatic increase in stamp duty came only months before the Brexit vote. So it is very difficult to allocate 'blame' for falling house prices,

---

[27] Is it possible to have a rational debate about housing?, by Eamonn Butler,

especially in London, where prices and therefore stamp duty rises were highest. Remainers tend to blame Brexit; leavers tend to blame the stamp duty rise.

It's the Supply, stupid

There is an elephant in the room, which only seems to noticed by libertarian free marketeers: supply. Changing taxes, interest rates, immigration numbers, or future uncertainties do *not automatically* result in too little or too much housebuilding.

In a normal free market economy, supply keeps up with demand. If prices rise because e.g. more people want to live there, developers see opportunity, and start building. When demand is satisfied, prices fall again. Under perfect competition between house builders, with no unfair advantage given to any, their profit ratios would never be too excessive, as other builders would outcompete them. There would never be an over- or under-supply of houses; and prices wouldn't fluctuate much.

Why has supply not kept up with demand? Ever since the Town and Country Planning Act was introduced in 1947, house building is regulated to an extraordinary degree. Developers need to jump through many hoops before they can actually supply new houses to market.

There is no free market supply for housing anymore. House building is rendered numb by regulation. Even though many factors are responsible for the high building costs, the political decisions dwarf the other factors in significance. House building costs in Britain are among the highest in the world, with more than 35% of the cost attributable to regulation[28].

Overregulation has brought a shortage of housing and rapidly rising prices. Before the 1947 Country Planning Act nationalised planning, house prices fluctuated very little in the United Kingdom. Countries with much more liberal building rules have little fluctuation in house prices today, e.g. in Japan and Houston. The highest annual private house building in the UK took place in the 1930s.

In built-up areas such as London where building has a greater effect on the nearby voters, regulation and political interference with house building

---

Adam Smith Institute Blog, 8 January 2013.
[28]The impact of supply constraints on house prices in England, by Hilber and Vermeulen, Economic Journal, 30 July 2012.

reaches very high levels. Londoners will all have heard of battles to prevent new constructions. The countryside has large numbers of nimbys too: nobody wants to lose his view of the sun setting over a green field. Nobody seems to want new neighbours - it does not dawn on many people that unless more houses are built next to them, their own grandchildren will never be able to own one.

Both in urban and in rural areas, the reason to object to new houses is at least partially financial: if the area next to your house is built up, your property probably reduces in value. The Town and Country Act does not provide for compensation in the case of private financial loss resulting from development; and so neighbours are encouraged to block any development near them at any cost.

For more than three decades the UK has built fewer houses that any other European country. France and Germany typically build between 50 and 70 new units per 10,000 inhabitants. In the UK the numbers are below 40. The British housing stock is the smallest in Western Europe when measured as total residential floor space divided by the number of households.

The wrong solutions

Stamp duty rises for high end properties and buy-to-lets

Responding to the public outrage over ever less affordable homes, George Osborne introduced two dramatic stamp duty increases in 2016. Firstly, expensive properties became subject to punitive stamp duty rates of up to 12%. George Osborne legitimised this by saying that 98 % of home buyers would henceforth pay less stamp duty; and that only only houses worth over £1 million would pay more. Secondly, an additional 3% stamp duty levy was introduced for those buying a second home. First-time buyers would thereby have a tax advantage as compared to those who already own another home.

The stamp duty rises have been an unmitigated disaster. Fewer people are interested in investing their savings in buy-to-let properties. This means that fewer are being built. Many hard-working people buy a second property as an income source for when they retire. If fewer do this, more will end up needing government handouts in old age.

Far fewer transactions are taking place: people just stay put. Sales fell by seven per cent nationally in 2016. This has led to a fall in revenue for the Treasury of about £1 billion. The slowing of house sales has also an effect on other aspects of the UK economy such as estate agents, lawyers, removal-men, decorators, etc.

There has been a persistent rumble of anger over the introduction of punitive stamp duty rates. Jacob Rees-Mogg MP, a Conservative member of the Treasury Committee, said: "Taxation ought to be about raising the revenue governments need – not the politics of envy."

Requisitioning houses

When residents had to be rehoused because the Grenfell Tower, went up in flames, left wing leader Jeremy Corbyn proposed to introduce emergency legislation to requisition homes left empty by 'the rich' nearby, to rehouse the victims.

The only time that houses have been requisitioned in Britain was during World War II. Jeremy Corbyn suggested using Compulsory Purchase Orders, under which land can be seized in the public interest, e.g. to widen a road. Using this for emergency housing is in fact illegal. In addition, it would be unsuitable as an emergency measure as the process may take up to two years. Finally, home owners need to be compensated, so requisitioning luxury flats would be unaffordable.

The idea that large numbers of houses are left empty (allegedly by foreign investors, to 'bank' them later, when prices have shot up), is largely a myth. Research[29] by the London School of Economics found that houses which are left entirely empty amount to less than 1 % of the housing stock. Most foreign-owned properties are rented out - overseas investors want income, too.

In any event, requisitioning 'empty' houses would not increase the total supply of houses. The requisitioning policy proposed by Mr. Corbyn is one of redistributing shortage.

Stopping foreign sales

Those lamenting the housing shortage often point the finger at foreigners snapping up scarce housing. A York University analysis suggests around 13% of new market housing was sold to overseas residents across London as a whole in the two years to March 2016.

---

[29]The role of overseas investors in the London new-build residential market, by Scanlon, Whitehead, etc, Homes for London, 2017.

Making sales to foreign buyers difficult or illegal would harm new housebuilding[30]. Many off-plan pre-sales are precisely to these foreign buyers. Without these pre-sales to foreigners, most developments would not take place: some banks require pre-sales to start lending for new developments; and developers reduce their own risk by selling in advance.

And what if foreigners own flats? Eventually they will sell them - and they will come back onto the open market for all to purchase.

Price limits on house price rises

In 2013, the Royal Institute of Chartered Surveyors (RICS) argued that there should be a limit on house price rises of 5 per cent per annum. If rises go beyond this limit, the authorities should put restrictions on the mortgages banks can offer.

There are several reasons why such a policy wouldn't work[31]. First of all, prices based on supply and demand instead of government diktat have an important signal function. When prices rise (e.g. because an area becomes more desirable), builders know that they should build there. If many do this, prices will stabilise. Secondly, if demand and therefore prices rise, but the law reduces the price one can obtain to 5 %, sellers will refuse to sell, and sit it out until they can enjoy the higher prices later. This is the same mechanism which invariably creates shortages when governments introduce price controls on consumer goods. Thirdly, if mortgages are restricted, for example the young will find it more difficult to get onto the housing ladder. They may turn to more risky alternative funding instead.

Fourth, but not last, the proposed measure seems another example of Regulatory Failure Spiral[32]: regulations introduced to fix other failures resulting from regulation, which fail themselves. After the banking crisis the Bank of England made it more difficult for banks to lend through onerous capital requirements. Then there was an attempt to fix the resulting slump in the economy through quantitative easing: money printing. This devalued money and inflated property prices. Concerned about the extension of mortgage credit, the government regulates mortgages. When fewer people

---

[30]The role of overseas investors in the London new-build residential market, by Scanlon, Whitehead, etc, Homes for London, 2017.
[31]Artificially limiting rises in house prices will do more harm than good, by Philip Booth, Institute of Economic Affairs, 18 September 2013.
[32] Heavens on earth, how to create mass prosperity, by JP Floru, Biteback 2013.

can obtain a mortgage, the government starts guaranteeing mortgages, e.g. via the Help to Buy scheme, to people who would not normally have obtained a mortgage under normal market conditions (this is what set off the 2008 Financial Crisis in the first place: the US government helping to grant mortgages to people who were not able to afford it under normal market conditions). On top of that the government regulates and restricts planning to such an extent that house building is essentially rationed. The shortage continues to lead to even higher property prices. We have now had a decade of stagnation of real incomes, but property prices continue to sky-rocket.

Then this limit on house price rises is proposed to fix the above. How above getting rid of the previous failing government actions first?

Help to Buy scheme

In order to increase home ownership among the young, the government introduced various Help to Buy schemes. These did indeed drive up home ownership among the young. It also drove up demand for starter homes. At the same time, it barely increased the supply, as land continued to be rationed. It is estimated that Help to Buy pushed up house prices by an average of £8,000. Increasing demand when the supply is inelastic (over-regulated house building) always causes a price rise.

Moreover, past financial history teaches us that the decision of who obtains a mortgage and who doesn't, should be left to private sector decisions and private sector risk taking. When the US government started to guarantee mortgages through its government sponsored enterprises Fannie Mae and Freddie Mac, it went hopelessly wrong when it transpired that many of those who thus got a mortgage, were unable to repay it. This resulted in the 2008 Banking crisis.

How to stabilise house prices to normal levels

In a perfect market situation, the interaction between supply and demand would ensure that there is never a great shortage of surplus of housing. This supply and demand chain has been broken by government interference. To restore it, the state needs to back off house building, and let the market get on with doing what it does best: cater for the demand.

Reduce unaffordable regulation

The easiest method to fix the housing shortage is to liberate supply. Reducing the weight of regulations which affect the cost of building would go a long way towards building the millions of houses we need to bring house prices back to affordable levels. There are many options, and it would be best to implement as many as possible of these.

- More liberal zoning: becoming less prescriptive as to what sort of development can be done on which land;
- loosening up the greenbelt around London by selling off land which is of little ecological value;
- becoming less dogmatic about new house building on greenfields - after all, all built-up land was once greenfield; if building had been illegal we would be living in caves;
- cost assess building regulations and introduce a reasonableness test to make them apply (or not).

We need to be less prescriptive as to what sort of dwellings can be built. We have micromanagement rules to prevent 'tiny slums': e.g. rules on how many bedrooms new flats should have, and of what size. These are unhelpful in that it prevents developers from catering for market demand. For those who earn little, there may be no housing at all - and so we have seen the proliferation of overcrowded flats, 'beds in sheds', and homelessness. Preventing slums has led to worse slums. Many young people would jump at the opportunity to buy a micro flat[33].

Roll back 'green' rules: over recent years environmental legislation has dramatically increased building costs. This goes from insulation requirements arising from the Climate Change Act; to having to build expensive bat houses to house the two bats which were discovered in the roof of the house to be knocked down; or having to pay for expensive environmental reports to prove that there are no endangered newts in the infinitely small pond which will be left in place (!) next to the development.

Incentivise local authorities to approve development

Incentivising councils to approve building projects is another route which has barely been tried. At the moment, many building projects are thwarted, as nimbys have the upper hand. Politicians usually side with the nimbys, as they tend to be better organised than those who could profit from more

---

[33] Britain needs more slums, by Theo Clifford, Adam Smith Institute Blog, 2015.

homes being built. The nimbys typically live next to the proposed development: they will be aware of it; a lot is at stake. Those who could profit may not yet live in the area and are probably too busy saving up for a deposit.

Local authorities should be made to profit from housebuilding; perhaps by devolving part or all of property taxes to the local level (stamp duty, capital gains tax, business rates). Or councils could be given the right to purchase land (e.g. farm land); then grant it planning permission; and sell it on at the increased value[34]. This would be a tremendous incentive for politicians to support development as the income stream could subsidise the entire council. Turning one hectare of farmland into development land increases the value from £15,000 to £1 million per hectare.

Housing related public expenditure could also be devolved to the local level: if local social housing costs go up because the local authority does not allow enough houses to be built, then that local authority should pay for the social costs resulting from its policy.

Sell off public land

Public bodies such as the NHS Trusts, local councils, Transport for London, central government, and an assortment of other public bodies, own vast tracts of land for no purpose. On top of that, they could be creative: one could for example put railway lines in tunnels and build houses on top.

In 2016, the London Land Commission, chaired by Mayor of London Boris Johnson, published the first ever register of public land in London. It identified 40,000 sites across London with a capacity to deliver at least 130,000 homes. The Mayor of London had already disposed of surplus land held by the Greater London Authority.

Unfortunately, a process in the hands of politicians was bound to lead to yet more interference by politicians. Instead of simply ordering to sell off the land to developers, the Commission 'works with land owners to determine availability and to encourage the marketing of public land to obtain the best possible housing development for Londoners, rather than selling with no obligations.' So political goals are once again trumping market demand.

---

[34] Cash-strapped councils can count on planning reform, by Madsen Pirie, Adam Smith Institute, 5 July 2017.

Abolish the Town and Country Planning Act 1947

Another alternative would be to abolish the Town and Country Planning Act 1947, and to return to the pre-1947 situation.

Planning law was nationalised by the Labour government in 1947[35]. The Town and Country Planning Act 1947 introduced the necessity to obtain planning permission. From then onwards ownership alone was no longer sufficient to be allowed to develop land. Prior to this, land owners were restricted in what they could do with their land because neighbours could sue them for all sorts of reasons based on common law. Therefore developers tried to negotiate with the neighbours beforehand. They made private agreements which allowed for reasonable development.

Given that they tried to nationalise virtually everything else, it doesn't surprise that the Attlee government abolished the finely balanced private property rights which had developed in the centuries before, and replaced it with a statist system. Never mind that the old system had served this country exceedingly well: private house building in this country peaked at 350,000 units in the 1930s, *before* nationalisation. The pre-planning era presented us with the many magnificent Medieval, Tudor, Georgian, Victorian, and Edwardian townscapes we still admire today. The old system of developers and neighbours coming up with something that was mutually beneficial, was replaced by politicians and bureaucrats deciding what is best.

We have to be realistic. While it would be highly desirable and potentially very effective to abolish nationalised Planning Law, it is pretty certain that the political will to do this is almost entirely lacking.

How to promote home ownership

We have seen that not enough is being built: demand outstrips supply, thereby creating massive house price inflation. This increase the length of the social housing waiting list. But building social housing increases the price of private housing, which in turn makes the social housing waiting list longer again.

The few houses that are being built tend to be rentals. But isn't there tremendous societal value in private home ownership, as opposed to renting? Apart from the obvious safety and security and peace of mind of the

---

[35] What the Immigrant Saw, by JP Floru, Bretwalda Books 2011.

owners as opposed to the uncertainty of tenants, there is also: greater pride and care for the property; the property is a capital asset, which can be used to borrow against to buy another property or set up a business; not becoming a burden upon the state; the opportunity to leave a nest-egg to your children. All of these are clear conservative values.

Reduce stamp duty for all

So we need to encourage people to buy, rather than to rent. The government has tried to thwart buy-to-let by increasing stamp duty; especially for second homes. Stamp duty is now so high that more and more people just stay put, and build an extension instead. Though cheaper houses are subject to lower stamp duty rates, there is a 'clogging-up' factor: if a first time buyer stays put in his house because he will have to pay much more stamp duty for his next house, then that 'starter-house' will never come on the market for new first-time buyers, thereby increasing house prices for smaller properties. So taxing big houses reduces supply and increases the prices for first-time buyers. Stamp duty for first-time buyers is very low, but it has gone up. First-time buyers used to be exempt from paying stamp duty up to £250,000 - today it is £125,000. The solution is simple: stamp duty needs to go down for all categories of home buyers.

Turn Right to Buy into Right to Own

Margaret Thatcher's Right to Buy policy must rank among the most successful policies ever to have been introduced by a Conservative government. Social tenants were allowed to buy their home at market value, but reduced by a substantial discount of between 33 to 50 %, depending on the number of years the tenants lived there.

Right to Buy exists up to this day. Under David Cameron the discounts were increased. There is however a problem: as house prices have sky-rocketed, even at a substantial discount, they are unaffordable for most.

Allister Heath, who was the Editor-in-Chief of the CityAm newspaper at the time, came up with a new exciting proposal. Council houses should simple be *given away* to the tenants living there.

Social tenants, including those housed by Housing Associations, who have been in work for the past year, should be gifted their council home. Pensioners would be automatically eligible. In return, recipients would cease to receive housing benefit. The state could claw back some of the money when it is sold, depending on the number of years the new owner stayed put. So if the new owner sells at a healthy profit after just three years, he would be subject to, say, a 50% tax on the sale value. If he stays for much longer, it could be less. The giveaway would not be much greater than the discounts enjoyed under Right to Buy - but social tenants could become owners without a deposit.

Social tenants in 4.1 million homes would become home owners.

'A New Form of Politics': Brexit, Immigration and the rise of Populism in Europe

-- by James F. Downes, Director of British & European Politics for Parliament Street; and Christopher Hanley, Director of Public Opinion & Polling for Parliament Street

Introduction

Despite the efforts of a large part of the Government and the Remain camp through their strategy of outlining economic risks associated with Brexit, on the 23rd June 2016 Britain voted to leave the European Union (EU) by a margin of 52-48%. In order to achieve a better understanding of why the majority of British voters decided to leave the EU we need to first trace the historical processes of what we call in this chapter, 'British Exceptionalism'. Drawing on original polling data from Eurobarometer surveys, this chapter examines the attitudes of the British public towards membership of the EU compared to European citizens taken as a whole from 1973-2016. The data are then broken down across decades in order to examine variations in support for the EU amongst the British public. The central argument of this article is that Britain has always been a 'reluctant' member of the EU.

Against this backdrop, the chapter then turns to investigate the increasing politicisation and salience of immigration in British politics since 2005 and how immigration became the central issue that dominated the EU Referendum outcome in 2016. The third and final section then outlines how the immigration issue has also driven support for populist radical right parties in both France (Front national) and Germany (Alternative für Deutschland). With Brexit a reality, the chapter will outline how this anti-establishment insurgency has direct implications for the upcoming French, German and Dutch Elections in 2017.

'The Reluctant Europeans': British Exceptionalism from 1973-2016

From the start, Britain's membership of the European Union was controversial, both domestically and internationally amongst fellow European neighbours.[36] The French President Charles de Gaulle frequently vetoed British membership throughout the 1960's. Yet, despite the challenges, the United Kingdom finally became a member of the EU in 1973 under Ted Heath's Conservative Government with the Labour Party split on the issue.

Taking 1973 as our benchmark, this section provides an overview of public perceptions amongst the British public towards the EU and draws on trend data from the Eurobarometer (conducted by Kantar Public) from 1973-2016 that allows us to track changes in public opinion across roughly each decade of membership (1973-1980, 1981-1990, post-1990, 2000 onwards). The question that we examine asks survey respondents the following: "Generally speaking, do you think the United Kingdom's membership of the EU is a good or bad thing?" A random sample of survey respondents across the country was asked this question roughly twice a year from 1973-2011, providing us with an uninterrupted trend series across time. The time series trend starts in September 1973 and is represented in Figure 1.1 below.

Legend
Each of the following trendlines within this chapter displays the data in the same way. The **dark blue** and **dark red** lines represent the UK results for this question. The **light blue** and **light red** lines represent the average of all EU Member States. Other EU Member States were of course asked about their own country's membership of the EU.

'A good thing' (EU average result, with countries being asked about their own EU membership)
'A good thing' (UK result)

'A bad thing' (UK result)
'A bad thing' (EU average result)

The fact that the dark blue line, *which represents the proportion of British respondents who think that membership is a good thing,* is consistently lower than the lighter blue line, *representing attitudes in the rest of the EU,* goes to show that Brexit should not have come as a surprise: Britain has always

---

[36] The European Union in its earliest form was known as the European Economic Community (EEC) and can be seen as a precursor to the European Union which incorporated the European Communities in 1993.

been a reluctant member, sporting an approval rating of 20 percentage points lower than the European average.

Figure 1.1: Attitudes towards Britain's Membership of the EU (1973-2011)

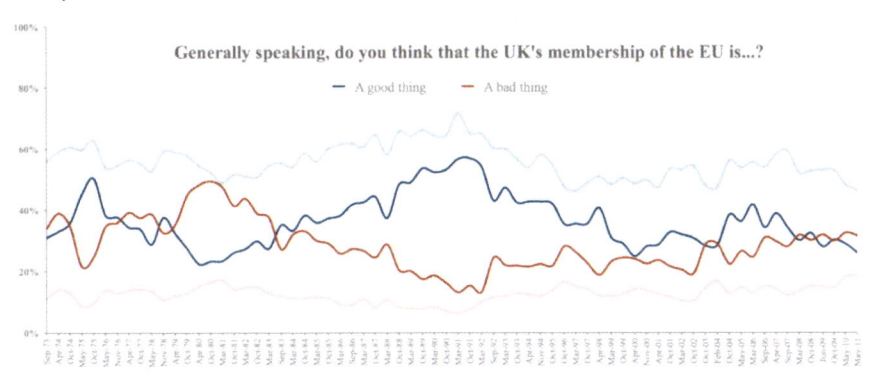

Generally speaking, do you think that the UK's membership of the EU is...?

The early years (1973 – 1980)

The first period (1973-1980) shows the UK reaching its lowest result on record, with the proportion of people who think membership is a good thing hovering just above the 20% mark at the end of the decade. This suggests from the very start that the UK was a reluctant member of the EU, and it was was viewed by the public largely as a government-led venture with very little popular support. These low results likely reflected early forms of Euroscepticism that formed as a consequence of years of membership rejection by other EU Member States, and the negative press that covered it. The 20% approval and 50% disproval provides a stark contrast to the EU average result (with the lighter colours) which is much more positive and shows general support for the European project.

In 1974, shortly after coming to office, Labour Prime Minister Harold Wilson promised to put the issue of EU membership to the British people in a referendum.[37] The final result was overwhelmingly in favour of staying in, with 67% voting to continue membership in June 1975. Interestingly, the period surrounding the referendum also saw a large bounce in the polls with regard to the UK's European membership, likely as a result of the

---

[37] Helm, Toby. "British Euroscepticism: A Brief History." The Guardian. 7th February 2016. Date Accessed: 1st September 2016.
https://www.theguardian.com/politics/2016/feb/07/british-euroscepticism-a-brief-history

Government's campaign to remain. However, shortly after the referendum the positive result, which came as a surprise to the European project, proved to be no more than a poll bounce or a blip, with the years of 1975-1980 seeing results return to their normal levels of overwhelming Euroscepticism.

Figure 1.2: Attitudes towards Britain's Membership of the EU (Period 1: 1973-1980)

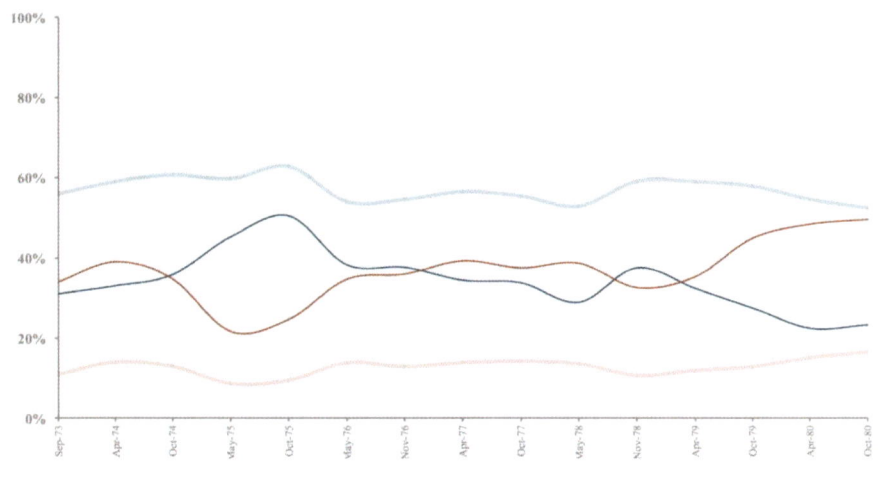

New hopes for the European project (1981 – 1990)

This decade was arguably one of the most important in forming what the British public have now come to associate with the EU. The early years first witnessed enlargement to some of the Mediterranean countries, such as Spain, Portugal and Greece – which have all since experienced numerous economic issues with handling their national debt amidst the recent Eurozone crisis. Shortly afterwards Thatcher negotiated a rebate on the UK's contribution to the EU budget, which continued to feed into rhetoric about EU mismanagement.

Perhaps most importantly, the Schengen Agreement was signed in 1985, creating the borderless zone across the continent. The UK managed to negotiate an opt-out of the treaty, and yet despite this, the concept of free movement and uncontrolled migration continued to fuel the anti-EU perspective. The Single European Act was signed in 1986, which sought to create a single market by 1992.

Against the backdrop of a rapidly developing EU, the 1980s also coincided with a dramatic shift in Conservative and Labour Party attitudes towards Europe. Figure 1.3 breaks down perceptions amongst the British public from

1981-1990. During this period, the time trend highlights two key points in history. Firstly, the European outlook steadily improved, achieving higher levels of support for the European project than ever seen before.

Secondly, the EU and the UK both witnessed a similar trend and shows support coalescing in public opinion. A key event during this period was Thatcher's Bruges speech[38] in 1988 which outlined a Eurosceptic vision of Europe, and her worry that the original vision of Europe as a trading area would be extended to an ever greater political and economic union. During the same period, Neil Kinnock's Labour Party shifted from its Eurosceptic stance in the 1970's towards supporting the European project. However, this period also saw Kinnock face increasing pressure from the left wing of his party.

Despite Thatcher's efforts to put on the brakes, for the first time the prospects for a happy relationship with the EU started to look good. The UK managed to opt out of signing the Schengen Agreement, alleviating the security concerns of the Government and the public, and Thatcher also negotiated a significant rebate on the UK's contribution. Positive developments within the EU and the achievements of the British government to safeguard British interests are reflected in a steady improvement of British opinion. Overall, events during this period suggested that the EU was prepared to listen to the UK and make compromises in order to keep it as a member.

---

[38] Helm, Toby. "British Euroscepticism: A Brief History." The Guardian. 7th February 2016. Date Accessed: 1st September 2016.
https://www.theguardian.com/politics/2016/feb/07/british-euroscepticism-a-brief-history

Figure 1.3: Attitudes towards Britain's Membership of the EU (Period 2: 1981-1990)

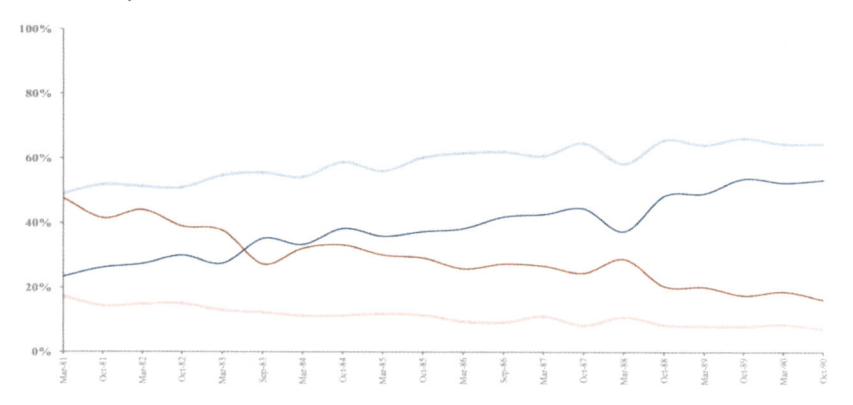

Post-1990s slump

This growing optimism among the British public was short-lived and was met with an equally steady decline in perceptions, sinking once again to the low levels witnessed in the 70's. Positive perceptions of the EU reached their 40-year peak in the UK in 1990. Figure 1.4 shows a steady decline in public opinion, both across the EU but is particularly pronounced in the UK.

Events in this period proved to be tumultuous with Thatcher's downfall and the European Exchange Rate mechanism collapse in 1992, alongside the creation of the modern day EU from the Maastricht Treaty. During this period John Major's Government faced frequent division over Europe with a number of Eurosceptic cabinet members, including notable figures such as Michael Portillo and John Redwood, voicing their dissent. At the same time, Tony Blair's rebranding of New Labour coincided with the party committing itself to the EU and the prospect of greater integration and enlargement in the future.[39]

New Labour's shift to the centre ground and new-found dedication to integration capitalised on the warming of British citizens towards the European project, but at the same time stood in stark contrast to the Government's position over the preceding decade. By the end of Thatcher's tenure, the Tories had replaced Labour as the party of Euroscepticism, even

---

[39] Helm, Toby. "British Euroscepticism: A Brief History." The Guardian. 7th February 2016. Date Accessed: 1st September 2016.
https://www.theguardian.com/politics/2016/feb/07/british-euroscepticism-a-brief-history

as her own downfall within her party was most likely triggered by her opposition to Mr Delors' social EU plans in her speech in Bruges.

The ejection from the European exchange rate mechanism and the signing of the Maastricht treaty provided the British tabloids with fresh anti-EU ammunition, which in turn contributed to the weakening of trust and opinion among the general public. Thatcher's resignation in 1990 arguably also marked the end of strong resistance towards the encroaching EU, giving way to a weaker John Major who was relieved of his power shortly after in 1997.

Figure 1.4: Attitudes towards Britain's Membership of the EU (Period 3: 1991-2000)

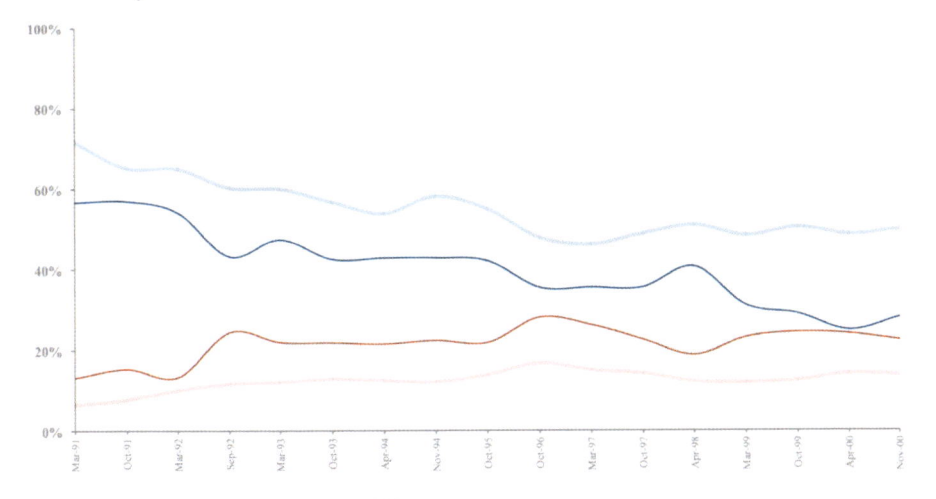

Brexit beats recovery (2000-2016)

The millennial period saw a slight recovery in public perceptions surrounding the UK's place in the EU and Figure 1.5 depicts this relationship. The '90s witnessed the positive perception of EU membership spiral downwards from around the 60% mark to 30%. This began to level off around the same time that Blair took office in 1997. However it is also worth highlighting that two years after his re-election in 2003, negative perceptions again overtook the positive.

To provide some perspective, the general view of EU membership amongst the public had been more positive than negative for the previous 20 years (since 1983).[40] From an EU-wide perspective, the UK was the only country to witness levels as low as this: in all other Member States, positive perceptions historically always outweighed the proportion with negative views.

When Gordon Brown took office in 2007, he was met with one of the largest financial crises Europe had seen; this unsurprisingly was a big blow for the European project. The end of the decade saw Euroscepticism on top, reigniting the Eurosceptic wing within the Conservative Party as well as giving momentum and much needed credibility to the United Kingdom Independence Party (UKIP), which gained significant traction in the European Parliament election in 2009.[41]

Movements in British public opinion virtually mirrored those observed on the continent but despite this, views on both sides of the channel never converged. Positive opinion of the EU in the UK had consistently trailed by 20 percentage points since the UK joined the community in 1973. The European average on the other hand very rarely saw opinion levels sink past the 50% mark. This reflects the general attitude the UK has had since it joined. The relationship was always assessed on the basis of checks, balances, benefits and costs, whereas Britain's European counterparts had invested on a more emotional level.

Figure 1.5: Attitudes towards Britain's Membership of the EU (Period 4: 2001-2011)

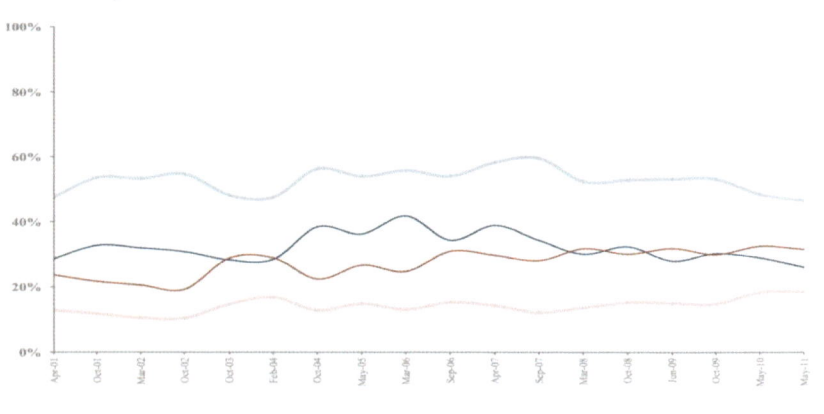

---

[40] Helm, Toby. "British Euroscepticism: A Brief History." The Guardian. 7th February 2016. Date Accessed: 1st September 2016.
https://www.theguardian.com/politics/2016/feb/07/british-euroscepticism-a-brief-history
[41] Ford, Robert. & Goodwin, Matthew (2014). Revolt on the right: Explaining support for the radical right in Britain. Routledge.

The European Commission decided to stop asking the question about EU membership after 2011 so we turn to a new question which similarly gauges public opinion. This question asked whether the EU conjured up a positive or a negative opinion for respondents. There was also a 'neutral' option but for the sake of clarity, this is not presented in the trendline below.

Figure 1.6 shows that the UK not only trailed behind the overall EU trend in terms of sentiment but the British public also reacted in a much more negative way in 2011. This year saw many countries re-enter recession, as well as disputes around various bailout packages. David Cameron assumed office in 2010 and arguably used the gradual recovery of the British economy against the backdrop of the failing European economy as a reason for offering the British public a referendum on membership of the EU. Furthermore, in a speech about the future of the EU at Bloomberg in 2013, Cameron also outlined fundamental problems about the democratic deficit problem within the EU, in the lack of representation and accountability provided to ordinary citizens.[42] This eventually became part of his platform in 2015 to appease the Eurosceptics inside his own party and seek to ameliorate the threat of UKIP's electoral advance on the EU issue.

The 2015 general election also provided the Conservatives with a credible victory over the Labour Party and as part of Cameron's pledge, a referendum on the EU was legislated for and eventually held. Interestingly, during the same period and for the first time in history, British and European public opinion alike effectively converged in their view towards the EU (if we observe the proportion who have a positive opinion in Figure 1.6).

However, it should be highlighted that a rise was also witnessed in negative perceptions of the EU in the run up to the referendum amongst the British public. As mentioned, respondents on this question could also answer that they had a neutral opinion. In the final months, the number of those who said that they were neutral rapidly decreased as the general public were effectively forced to form an opinion on the issue. From the figure below, it is clear that those sitting on the fence were better mobilised by the Brexit campaign, since the 'negative opinion' grew at a much faster rate from 2015.

---

[42] Cameron, David. "EU speech at Bloomberg." Bloomberg. 23rd January 2013. Accessed: 5th January 2017.
https://www.gov.uk/government/speeches/eu-speech-at-bloomberg

Although Figure 1.6 seems to suggest that British public opinion appeared to improve in the final months, years and years of ingrained British Euroscepticism eventually prevailed on the 23rd June. Evidently, Britain has always been a 'reluctant' member of the EU and this phenomenon can be viewed as 'British Exceptionalism'.

Figure 1.6: Attitudes towards the EU in general (2002-2016)

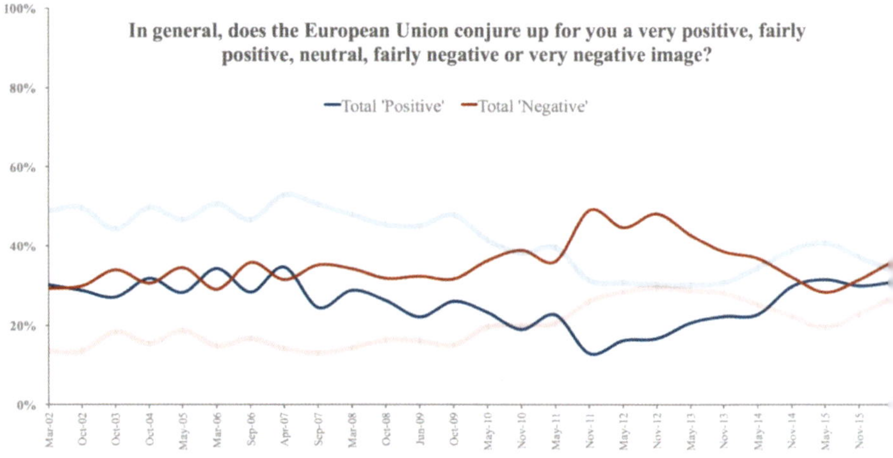

III - Salience of the Immigration issue across the continent

One key issue that has gained significant traction in both the UK and countries across the EU is the topic of immigration. Recent years have seen a number of hard-hitting terrorist attacks and perhaps most significantly, the EU as an institution has failed in its handling of the refugee crisis. With no effective common foreign and security policy, the EU was unable to react effectively to the crisis in the Mediterranean and was consequently scolded by national press across the continent.

The Eurobarometer asks respondents across the EU several questions that are relevant to this topic. One question that is particularly pertinent asks respondents what they think are the two most important issues facing their country. Europeans were provided with around 15 answer options to choose from, ranging from taxation to pensions, and immigration to terrorism. Focussing only on the proportion of people who selected immigration, it is clear from the figure below that the UK has always stood apart.

Of the 15 or so answer options, immigration has always been chosen by around 30% of people in the UK, rising to 44% in November 2015. At the same time, an additional quarter of respondents selected terrorism as one of the leading concerns for the country. Overall, it seems that more than half of British people are concerned about either of the two issues and this has been a consistent trend since the question was first put to the general public in 2005.

By contrast, immigration has been much less of an issue for the two other leading powers in the EU: France and Germany. Despite being proponents of the Schengen Area which allows for the free movement of EU citizens, the proportion of people in each of the countries that consider immigration as one of the main problems has historically been considerably lower than in the UK. However, it is worth noting that in recent years, and likely as a result of Merkel's open-door policy in response to the refugee crisis, Germans have increasingly considered immigration as the main issue facing the country.

Figure 2.1: Most important issue facing country: immigration (2005-2016)

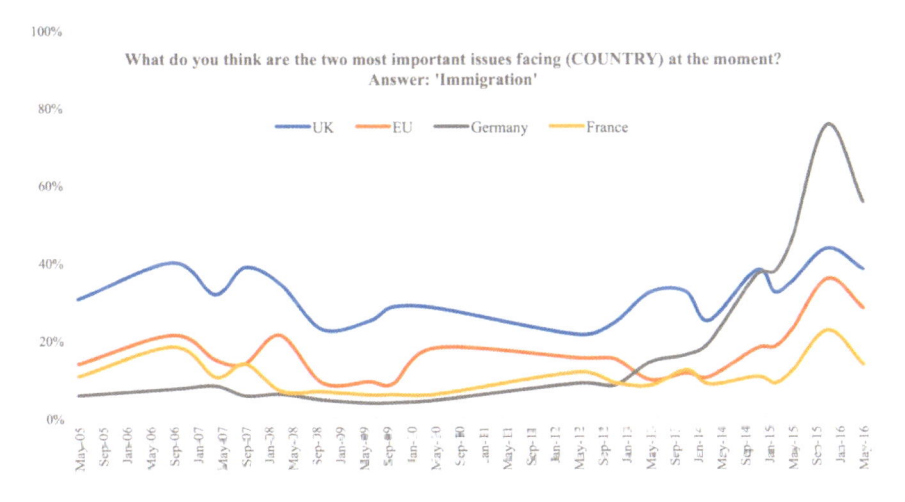

For Germany, free movement across the continent is no longer restricted to EU citizens but now includes refugees and migrants escaping wars in the Middle-East. Traditionally, Germany was considered a safe haven but recent terrorist attacks have eroded the initial welcoming attitude. To a lesser extent, the same trend is also taking place in France. Although France did not subscribe to the open-door policy, terrorist attacks – implicitly associated with immigration in public discourse – are becoming an increasing concern. In May 2016, around 30% of people in France and Germany considered terrorism as one of the main problems facing their country.

Figure 2.2: Most important issue facing country: terrorism (2005-2016)

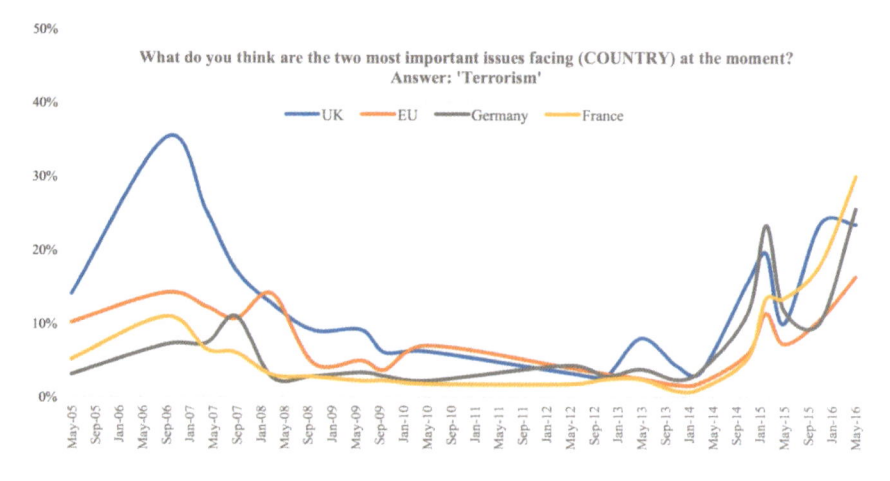

In the UK, UKIP has arguably managed to capitalise on these rising concerns and at the same time has taken ownership of the anti-establishment mood. MPs in both the Labour and Conservative Parties are divided on where they stand on the EU.[43] The divisions run deep through their history. Up until 1990, the Labour Party had traditionally been the party that opposed EU integration, but the Tories took their place as New Labour came to the fore. Thatcher, who valued traditional conservative ideals above a closer European economic union, dragged the Conservative Party to the 'soft' Eurosceptic platform they are known for today. UKIP on the other hand are clear in their objectives and have used their success in European elections to further their 'hard' Euroscepticism and cause for leaving the EU. Immigration, as shown in Figure 2.2, is clearly a big topic in today's political discourse and will only continue to pose an issue for national governments in the EU. On top of that, trust in political institutions at both the national and EU level is generally low and has weakened over the past 15 years, likely as a result of the lingering economic crises and involvement in foreign wars.

Responsibility for immigration: EU vs. National Government

---

[43] Goodwin, M., & Milazzo, C. (2015). UKIP: Inside the campaign to redraw the map of British politics. Oxford University Press.

Not only are immigration and terrorism contentious issues in modern day politics, but there is much disagreement in the EU about where responsibility should lie. Data from the Eurobarometer show that the UK also stands out in this regard (Figure 2.3).

The Eurobarometer provides EU respondents with a number of policy areas and asks them whether decisions related to it should be made by the national government or the EU. Here, we will focus on the results for immigration policy and although the question was last asked in 2011, the results are still interesting to discuss. Taking the EU as a whole, almost two thirds (60%) think that decisions regarding immigration policy should be made jointly with the EU. In France, this figure stands at 70% and in Germany, 64%. It is clear that on the continent, European citizens want the EU to legislate and be involved in immigration matters; only a minority think that decisions regarding immigration policy should be dealt with solely at the national government level.

Bucking the trend, the UK holds the opposite view. In contrast, two thirds of British citizens think that decisions to do with immigration policy should be made by the national government only. Figure 2.3 shows that only 32% of respondents thought that immigration should be coordinated with the EU. This is perhaps unsurprising given the UK's unique position outside of the Schengen Area but since immigration played such a large role in mobilising Brexit support, this view proved to be play an influential role on the 23rd June.

Figure 2.3: Responsibility for immigration (2011)

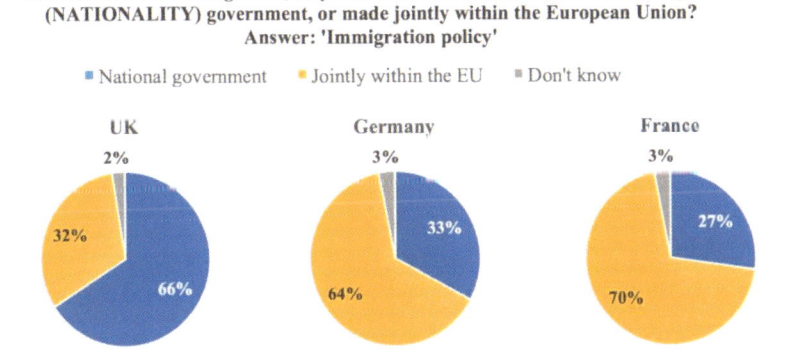

For each of the following areas, do you think that decisions should be made by the (NATIONALITY) government, or made jointly within the European Union?
Answer: 'Immigration policy'

■ National government   ■ Jointly within the EU   ■ Don't know

	UK	Germany	France
National government	66%	33%	27%
Jointly within the EU	32%	64%	70%
Don't know	2%	3%	3%

How EU immigration is viewed

As part of their bi-yearly Standard Eurobarometer survey, the European Commission asks the general public what their opinion is of immigration of people from other EU countries, with an answer scale ranging from very positive to very negative (Figure 2.4). Turning first to the results of Germany and France, we can find that a majority of people have an overall positive opinion of intra-EU immigration. Figure 2.4 shows that in Germany, the proportion who are in total positive is at 62% while in France it is 56%. Taking the EU as a whole, around 57% of people share this opinion.

In the UK however, a minority of people have a positive view of immigration of EU citizens to the EU, with a share of 48% in May 2016 and in November 2014, this proportion was as low as 42%. This shows once again that the British outlook differs from majority opinion on the continent. And while the difference between the UK and France is not huge on this matter – just 8 percentage points – it has proved to be significant when a decision such as Brexit was made with just a 4 point margin (52% Leave vs. 48% Remain).

Figure 2.4: Attitudes towards the immigration of people from other EU Member States (2016)

Please tell me whether each of the following statements evokes a positive or negative feeling for you. Answer: 'Immigration of people from other EU Member States'

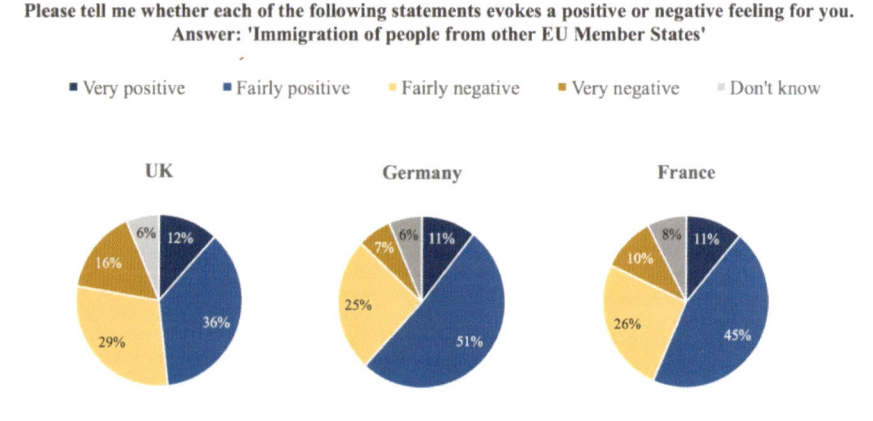

- Very positive
- Fairly positive
- Fairly negative
- Very negative
- Don't know

UK: Very positive 12%, Fairly positive 36%, Fairly negative 29%, Very negative 16%, Don't know 6%

Germany: Very positive 11%, Fairly positive 51%, Fairly negative 25%, Very negative 7%, Don't know 6%

France: Very positive 11%, Fairly positive 45%, Fairly negative 26%, Very negative 10%, Don't know 8%

Rise in populism and declining levels of trust in institutions

The results and analysis thus far have shown how attitudes in the UK differ from the attitudes of people across the rest of the EU. The UK has historically been a reluctant member of the EU and immigration in particular was an issue that was able to effectively mobilise support for Brexit. UKIP is well known for its hard stance in this regard but it is also often labelled as a populist radical right party: one that is able to marshal the public against the government and the establishment. Similar movements are also gaining traction in other EU countries, such as France with the Front National. There are two indicators in the Eurobarometer that help us understand the anti-establishment sentiment in the EU: people's trust in the national government and their trust in the EU (Figure 2.5).

Looking firstly at trust in the national government, Figure 2.5 shows that the results are fairly low for the UK, France and Germany, as well across the EU in general. In all three countries, the share of people that 'tend to trust' their national government does not exceed 50%, and often hovers between the 20-40% mark. In France, and across the EU more generally, trust in the national government has seen a general decline over the past 15 years. In 2001, the share of people in the EU that trusted their government was around the 50% mark (48%) but this has steadily fallen over the years to just above a quarter at present (27%). In France, the deterioration is much more pronounced, in part due to the extremely low satisfaction levels for President François Hollande. The UK has witnessed a similar trend but since 2012, trust has significantly improved, now at 34% which is significantly higher than the EU average and France.

Figure 2.5: Trust in the national government (2001 – 2016)

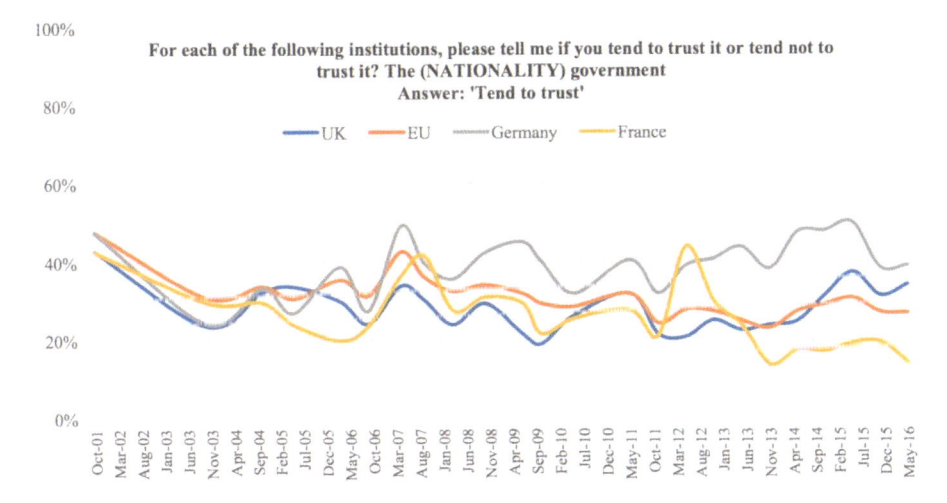

Trust in the national government has been shown to be fairly unremarkable across the EU and moreover, it seems to be in decline. And while people in the UK now seem to trust the current government more than their EU counterparts, it was often not that way. Overall, British trust in their government is not much different to the sentiment experienced on the continent. However, when one looks at the trust in the EU, a larger separation becomes apparent (Figure 2.6).

Across the EU, it seems that citizens are generally more trustful of the EU than they are of their government. In April 2007, the level of trust almost reached the 60% mark, following the enlargement of the Schengen Area to include several Central and Eastern European states. Germany, France and the EU overall have been historically aligned in their opinion of the EU. The UK on the other hand has been consistently more pessimistic towards the EU with trust ratings no less than 20 percentage points lower than elsewhere.

Figure 2.6 shows that over the past two years public opinion in the UK has converged with that on the continent. Between May 2014 and May 2016, trust almost doubled (from 16% to 30%), likely due to the increasing prospects of a referendum on the EU and the campaigning from the Remain camp. Nonetheless it is worth highlighting that the Leave camp won the referendum in a country where the level of trust in the EU is not currently far from the levels held elsewhere in the EU. Opinion levels do not seem to be improving either where there has been a steady downward trend since 2007 across the whole EU.

Figure 2.6: Trust in the EU (2003 – 2016)

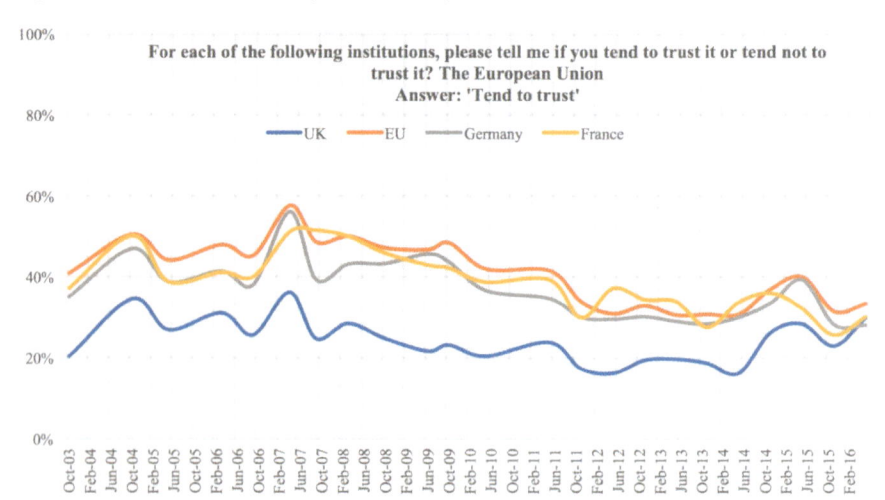

With the French, German and Dutch elections around the corner in 2017, dwindling trust in national governments and the EU will be of particular significance. Both Germany and France have been hit hard by terrorist attacks over the past few years. In France, the Front National led by Marine Le Pen is becoming more and more prominent as attitudes towards immigration have been harmed by the lingering refugee crisis and ongoing attacks. In Germany, Angela Merkel will be running for a fourth term and while her approval ratings are still fairly high, they have arguably been damaged by the terrorist attacks, which have become more associated with her open-doors policy.

IV- Conclusion

This chapter has shown that one of the main drivers of Britain leaving the European Union was immigration, given its increased politicisation in British politics. It is clear that politicians on both the left and right of British politics have failed to recognise the long-term impact of British Euroscepticism amongst the British public. To borrow a theory from the political scientists Matthew Goodwin and Robert Ford, a large segment of people who voted for Brexit constituted the 'left behind' in society that comprises the traditional working class. We argue that politicians are in denial if they think that Brexit was a flash in the pan.[44] We are living in a 'new form of politics', not just in Britain, but in Europe more broadly. The relationship between elected representatives and voters has evolved and politicians are now under increasing pressure to stand up and deliver on their election promises.

In the run up to the EU Referendum on the 23rd June, political commentators outlined the potential political and economic uncertainties that may arise as a consequence of leaving the EU. Global economic volatility is likely with the decline in value of the British pound and further economic uncertainties.[45] Whilst debates over what Brexit will look like are likely to dominate the next two years of British politics, the EU is currently facing a three-pronged existential crisis.[46] Brexit is one element, another being the ongoing migration crisis and disputes among EU member states in resolving the

---

[44] Ford, Robert. & Goodwin, Matthew (2014). Revolt on the right: Explaining support for the radical right in Britain. Routledge.

[45] Downes, James. "To Brexit or not to Brexit." 英國"脫歐" 何去何從. The Chinese General Chamber of Commerce, Vision. http://www.cgcc.org.hk/en/chamber/bulletin/files/Bulletin_1465548781.92453_P.19-26.pdf Interview conducted in June 2016.

[46] Rankin, Jennifer. "EU is facing existential crisis, says Jean-Claude Juncker." The Guardian. 14th September 2016. Date Accessed: 1st September 2016. https://www.theguardian.com/world/2016/sep/13/jean-claude-juncker-eu-is-facing-existential-crisis

situation, an issue that the latest Eurobarometer data shows is increasing in salience among voters in France and Germany. Thirdly and most significantly, there has been a sharp decline in trust across European democracies towards the EU.[47]

Most significantly, the series of Eurobarometer data shows the increased importance of the immigration issue amongst French citizens, coupled with declining levels of support for the EU project in France. The data also demonstrate that in comparison to the UK, Germany and the Euro area average, French citizens' satisfaction with the EU has reached its lowest, and most importantly these findings pointed to a distinct lack of trust in the French Government led by President François Hollande. These results are have direct implications for the upcoming French Presidential and Legislative Elections in 2017. Populist radical right parties such as Alternative for Germany (AfD), the Front National in France and Geert Wilders' Party for Freedom (PVV) have achieved prominence of late by weaving a narrative of political discontent and 'hard' Euroscepticism.[48] With French, German and Dutch parliamentary elections on the horizon and the resurgence of far right populism, we are currently living in a 'new form of politics.' How the EU manages and responds to these events will determine much about its future state.

---

[47] Schmidt, V. A. (2015). The Eurozone's Crisis of Democratic Legitimacy. Can the EU Rebuild Public Trust and Support for European Economic Integration? (No. 015). Directorate General Economic and Financial Affairs (DG ECFIN), European Commission.
[48] Kriesi, H., & Pappas, T. S. (Eds.). (2015). European populism in the shadow of the great recession. ECPR Press.

The Brexit effect on the City: short term pain for long term economic gain
-- by Tim Focas, Director of Financial Services for Parliament Street

Introduction

"*I do not believe there is some fantasy world out there that if Britain leaves the EU we can somehow be economically better off*" – the words of former chancellor George Osborne, prior to June 23rd. But despite the falling value in Sterling since, GDP forecasts have consistently shown that Britain's economy hasn't slowed as much as first feared.

From the perspective of financial firms operating from the City, the only option is to be optimistic for the future. This is because ultimately, if the UK does not strike good deal for the City, then European financial markets will suffer as investment, jobs and growth will grind to a halt.

While there will clearly be initial costs to incur, notably passporting rights and seamless access to the Single Market, this paper argues why the long-term prospects are brighter than ever for the City.

Pre-negotiation niggles

Speculation has been rife since referendum that thousands of banking jobs across London are at risk. The likes of Goldman Sachs, JP Morgan, HSBC, and Citibank have all talked about jobs potentially moving to Paris Frankfurt and Dublin. Although, interestingly, none of these firm are to make any concrete announcements. Europe has also been on its own charm offensive to attract talent away from the City. Emmanuel Macron has wasted little time to outline his his plans to implement structural reforms to enable Paris to house key companies seeking to move operations away from London.

However, there has been a distinct lack of clarity about the nature of the jobs likely to move to mainland Europe. To date, only Lloyd's of London has confirmed that it will 100 jobs to new Brussels office. The biggest fear for financial firms like Lloyd's is, of course, losing the ability to buy and sell their services because of the loss of passporting rights. Even equivalence rules would not give firms the same sort of freedom they currently enjoy.

With the majority of financial institutions yet to make their position clear, and with Britain's future relationship with the Single Market uncertain, there has unsurprisingly been a few bumps in the road. As remainers keep harping on about, Sterling dropped 11 per cent in value in the immediate aftermath of the referendum, and though it has recently recovered somewhat, the pound has plunged to its lowest level since 1985. This has led many investors turning towards both the US dollar and the yen as relative safe havens.

There has also been a reduction in spending in the first quarter of this year which in turn, has slowed growth. Barclays predicts business confidence to drop even more as there are still plenty of unknowns regarding how Brexit will play out over the next two years. In its post-Brexit report, the bank also claims that savings accounts will dry up as consumption rises faster than income, and that consumer house and car buying will drop to two-year lows.

With so much uncertainty surrounding the negotiations and UK's medium term economic prospects, how does the City ensure it retains its position as Europe's leading financial centre against the will of the EU political elite?

The City's 'strong and stable' foundations

To quote the Tory election message, the answer is rooted in City of London 'strong and stable' foundations – which have been in place long before the formation of the EU. The City is, of course, vital to a well-functioning European financial market. Not only is It is the heart of investment banking and fund management, it is also a powerhouse for the insurance industry. These sectors contribute around 75 per cent of the UK's trade surplus in services – £62bn in 2014 or around 3.5 per cent of GDP. The figure rises to £71bn when the trade surplus for related professional services – legal services, accountancy and management consultancy – is included.

This makes the UK the world's biggest net exporter of financial services, accounting for 12 per cent of the UK's total exports. On top of this, the City is home to 250 international banks and is responsible for 17 per cent of all international bank lending – more than Paris, Frankfurt and Dublin. Overall, the UK has the world's fourth largest banking sector, the third largest insurance sector, and is second in the world for assets under management at £6.2trn. In 2013-14, the banking sector alone paid £21.4bn in corporation tax, income tax, national insurance and the bank levy. Overall, UK financial services pay £71bn in tax (11.5 per cent of all tax revenues) 14 and employ around 1.1m people.

But it is not just about the amount of money the City contributes to the treasury, London also accounts for well over 40 per cent of global foreign exchange (FX) turnover. To put this into context, one of the City's closest financial rivals is Switzerland – a country also outside the EU – accounts for around 3 per cent of global FX turnover. Like Sterling, the Swiss franc is used as a reserve currency around the world – currently positioned just behind the US dollar, Canadian dollar, yen, sterling and of course, the euro. As we witnessed this time last year following the SNB debacle, the strength of the Swiss franc has a huge impact on other currencies, including emerging ones, many of which are still to recover fully from this event. The point here is that if an important financial market influencer such as Switzerland remain a fiscal power outside a centralised political union, what will stop London?

Unlike Switzerland, the City offers the deepest pool of capital in the time zone between Asia and the United States, and London time is often quoted in international business settings. This logistical benefit is unique to the City and would not change regardless of the referendum result. Then there is the infrastructure factor. London's trading infrastructure means that any move of currency flow to mainland Europe would come at a huge cost. The links that connect electronic trading, which now accounts for over half of the daily $5.3trn FX market globally, are all in London. Therefore, any move from the UK to Europe would not be quick and would require infrastructure spending the likes of Paris and Frankfurt would be unable to commit to.

If the early stage posturing is anything to go by, certain unelected EU officials appear hell-bent on punishing the City to make a political point. The trouble is that an unfavourable deal for London will only serve to restrict buying and selling across the capital markets which will ultimately, have a negative impact on the wider European economy. With this in mind, the City, like it has always done, needs to explore ways to reinvent itself for a post-Brexit era. And while there will be doubters amongst the senior ranks of the major financial institutions, there is evidence to suggest that operating outside the Single Market will be best for London in the long term.

Why the EU has held the City back

Despite the pretence of promoting competition, the EU is a fundamentally anti-competitive and protectionist organisation. The Single Market is the internal market of a Customs Union which operates very high external trade barriers with the sole objective of reducing effective competition from overseas. Even within the Single Market, the EU favours large corporations and makes it virtually impossible for small new entrants to compete. And it is these smaller firms that, historically, provide the financial innovation that enable European markets but operate more effectively for the end investor. If KPMG's fintech report titled "10 reasons London is becoming the Fintech capital of the world"[49] is anything to go by, then much of this innovation will emanate from the City.

But with notable the exceptions of certain requirements under MiFID I and II, which aim to increase competition and transparency across financial markets, the EU has been doing its level best to restrict innovation. A study by New City Initiative[50] shows that the following EU regulations are 'stifling innovation at smaller firms and restricting competitiveness as their regulatory burden continues to grow':

- Alternative Investment Funds Markets Directive (AIMFD)
- Financial Transaction Tax (FTT)
- OECD Common Reporting Standards
- Solvency II
- Basel III

While the large financial firms, most of which backed remaining in the EU, welcome these regulations that prevent more nimble companies competing against them, this does not serve in the best interest of European financial markets. Unfortunately, the current political narrative from the European Commission is being dressed up as being in the UK's national interest. This simply isn't true. In fact, it is very much against the interests of the City's customers who will see even lower investment returns as the large firms swallow up the small firms so they can no longer compete against them.

Unfortunately, there are strong indications that the City may have to wait beyond the 2-year Lisbon Treaty timetable to free itself from these burdensome EU regulations.

Transitioning to a brighter future?

With less than 24 months to go until Britain official exits from Brussels, one can't help but feel that the 2017 election has been underpinned by the government's desire to buy more time to renegotiate Britain's new trading relationship with Europe.

---

[49] KPMG: http://www.kpmgtechgrowth.co.uk/fintechcapital/
[50] New City Initiative: http://www.newcityinitiative.org/news/

With French elections concluded, and German elections to come later this year, it is not hard to see why she and the rest of Europe may be thinking along these lines. After all, despite noises emanating from European officials, what meaningful discussions can really take place in a year that sees the three biggest net EU contributors all go to the polls. And should the meat of the negotiations only being next year, it is simply not realistic to think that the UK's divorce terms, let alone new trade agreements, can be agreed in line with the Lisbon Treaty's timescales.

One of the key political factors lurking underneath the snap election is the government's desire to strike transitional agreements. In short, although far more complex in practice, these agreements mean that the UK would avoid what certain businesses call an economic "cliff edge" by immediately entering close EU trading relationships as part of the European Economic Area (EEA). While this process should, in theory, be relatively uncomplicated, the vast scale and complexity of the agreements could mean that this transitional period lasts for up to two years, at the very least.

So why exactly, despite her tough negotiation objectives, might the government be quietly wanting a transitional deal? The answer: "it's the economy stupid". For starters, it would mean Britain would have unfettered access to the single market, so the UK could continue to sell its services unrestricted. This would be particularly beneficial to financial services, which accounts for over 10 per cent of UK GDP, as banks would retain passporting rights, meaning that staff would not have to immediately relocate to Frankfurt or Paris. And for those who think this sounds a lot like being in the EU, think again. The UK would not have any say or be bound by the rules of Single Market, although it would have to make budget payments.

But while this all makes short to medium term economic sense; transitional arrangements will also depend on the degree of co-operation from the EU27. It is in everybody's interests that any transitional arrangements are kept as short term as possible, no longer than is needed to bridge the gap between the UK's exit from the EU and the conclusion of any formal long-term trading agreement with the EU.

If, as seems possible, the EU is not interested in such an agreement, then the UK should exit from the EU immediately this becomes apparent. And should this be the case, the City should encourage the government to support the development of legally binding regulatory standards at a global level free from political interference – all with the objective of promoting global consistency and cooperation between regulatory authorities.

The City should also lobby the government to support the overseas expansion of UK financial services in the fastest growing regions of the global economy. Furthermore, the City should pressure ministers to introduce a flexible system of work permits for skilled workers that covers workers who are offered a job in the UK, and who are located in any country in the world outside the UK. But perhaps the most important collective task for the City in helping to achieve this outcome is to refuse to move business to Europe. Only with this objective achieved can financial firms of all sizes based in London look positively to what may lies ahead.

A much brighter future
Once the transitional period has concluded, and who know how long that will take, the City can then start look forward to brighter times.

To start with, take the aforementioned burden that has weighed so heavily on the shoulders of financial institutions – regulation. Outside the EU, banks will have more direct influence on domestic market structure, if only for the fact that they will have to deal with a single local regulator. From executing trades to selling financial products, the entire trading value chain is simplified by only having to report into one body setting the rules. The upshot of this is that financial experts will have far more say on how trading is carried out. After all, who understands how markets operate better – Brussels bureaucrats or brokers and traders?

Another plus point of having an economic arrangement free from political ties is being able to react faster to global market events and new rules. Take Basel III, a regulation that forces banks to hold capital in reserve to cope with periods of high market stress. Swiss banks have been far faster to adopt these rules than European counterparts. When it comes to market events, if there is a major announcement from say the US Fed, a non-Eurozone nation can respond quicker if it isn't waiting for the EU, which has to gather ideas and views from the different member states. And one word springs to mind when having to respect the demands of 27 other countries – complexity.

Despite these clear advantages around flexibility to react to change and having a greater say on laws, being free to think independently is the central benefit. Understandably, many firms are concerned that the EU will be cutting the UK out of the big decisions. However, this view fails to acknowledge how by being part of an independent nation, firms will have no choice but to think on their feet. And this thinking usually lead to the new innovative solutions that historically, are created out by the smaller, more disruptive players. After all, it is not as if they will have the super structures of the EU as a safety net. Therefore, a refocus on quality and efficiency of client service should emerge across the City. From being able to provide a local and individualised services that the market currently craves, to providing access to all global markets trading all different types of financial products, investment banks cannot underestimate the value of delivering a more rounded service.

And for those who may feel that realigning their business is a daunting prospect, look no further than what happened post the Big Bang of 1986. A prime example of how the City showed the flexibility and foresight to adjust to new market conditions, perhaps more successfully than any other European nation. With this in mind, Brexit may not quite be the economic fantasy George Osborne and others referred to pre-the referendum, but more a new alternative vision of the future for the City and that is as a World Financial Centre outside the over-regulated protectionist European Union.

Brexit, while bringing medium term economic concerns, provides a brilliant longer term opportunity for the UK financial services industry to again know its place in the world. And that is as a servant to the real economy – by oiling its wheels and helping to facilitate the economic transactions of individuals and companies in the UK and across the globe. In recent years, it has not performed this function at all well. Instead, it is more interested in its own profits and bonuses than in meeting its customers' real needs.

Me, Myself and AI

-- by Dean Russell, Digital Transformation Director at Parliament Street and Founder of epifny consulting

The rapid rise of technology means that, for the first time in human history, the future we face is indeed uncertain. The technologically driven "fourth industrial revolution" is happening around us, whether we like it or not. Artificial intelligence (AI) is set to be at the centre of the revolution, and the choices we make now, from government policy to business planning, could define the role the UK plays on the global stage for the next century.

Unlike the original Industrial Revolution, which emerged visibly around the UK through the growth of factories, manufacturing, and industry, forging new communities around us, this fourth Industrial Revolution will be silent and stealthy, driving more people to work from home on increasingly specialised activities in an evermore globalised economy. This (industrial) revolution will not be televised. Instead, it will happen while the television is busy watching us (probably while we are working on the sofa talking to our watches).

Despite the majority of the general discussion focusing on fears of AI causing people to lose jobs and uncertainties around a post-work world, the considerations have to go much deeper. There are genuine ethical, moral, and societal concerns that we should also be discussing right now.

There are prominent voices with extreme concern about the risks of blindly walking into an AI-driven future. People ranging from Tesla visionary Elon Musk to Professor Stephen Hawking have all stated their fear that artificial intelligence could lead to the end of humanity. Musk, for example, has publicly spoken about the risks of what he calls technological singularity: the point at which machines will be sufficiently smart enough to redesign themselves to be even smarter and hence, see no need for *dumb* humans to exist.

While these fears need to be addressed, we can't ignore the fact the AI's ship has already left the port. So, we must explore the tremendous opportunities AI can bring to the UK. Perhaps instead of taking jobs, AI will in reality be more mundane in the mid-term, doing tasks humans just can't do.

The health sector is one such area where this principle applies. Huge leaps have been made by using AI to analyse and predict the onset of disease or to identify injuries. For example, just recently, there have been reports ranging from news about the improved prediction of Alzheimer's[51] to articles on AI providing advanced analysis[52] of x-rays and samples of diseased tissues. In the latter article The Guardian reported on the NHS England Expo where Prof Sir Bruce Keogh stated: "All of this [AI] takes us into a very new territory, and it's not a long way over there, it's actually here now".

While, understandably, there will be those who feel this is the first move in creating a workforce of robotic doctors, the reality is more likely to be improved prediction analysis behind-the-scenes in laboratories. There is no denying that data is becoming as much part of healthcare as the petri dish or the bandage; this is only going to increase in scale and importance. For example, according to recent research in Information Age[53], 60% of all medical information that has ever been generated was done so in the last six years alone. This figure is no doubt only going to rise especially with the increased use of devices such as the Apple Watch, which is becoming as much about health as it is about technology. We will need AI to help us take advantage of the insights this impossibly immense amount of data can bring.

Opportunities for positive intervention via AI have the chance to save lives, but we also need to have an open discussion about how we can apply this insight. In policing, for example, Forbes recently wrote about several UK law enforcement agencies dabbling in predictive policing[54]. A case study was shared from Durham, England, where they use a system called HART (Harm Assessment Risk Tool), which classifies individual offenders ranked by the probability that they will commit another offence in the future. While this test run seemingly worked out relatively accurately, other examples elsewhere have shown that some instances of AI have unexpectedly displayed signs of racial and gender bias, so AI may not be as impartial as some may hope[55].

The question is where the use of AI will end and how and where we decide to apply its a judgement. For example, research is already underway to develop artificial intelligence programs designed for the legal world. A researcher at the University of Alberta, Randy Goebel, is already working

---

[51] New Scientist: https://www.newscientist.com/article/2147472-ai-spots-alzheimers-brain-changes-years-before-symptoms-emerge/
[52] Guardian: https://www.theguardian.com/society/2017/sep/12/patients-illnesses-could-soon-be-diagnosed-by-ai-nhs-leaders-say
[53] Information Age: www.information-age.com/ai-hype-reality-healthcare-123468637/
[54] Forbes: https://www.forbes.com/sites/bernardmarr/2017/09/19/how-robots-iot-and-artificial-intelligence-are-transforming-the-police/#d640d6c5d61d
[55] ARS Technica UK: https://arstechnica.co.uk/science/2017/04/princeton-scholars-figure-out-why-your-ai-is-racist/

with Japanese researchers to create an AI that can pass the bar exam. He argues that search engines like Google are already commonplace in the courts, so artificial intelligence is the next logical step. This may be the case, but the process must surely include a discussion of where the distinction between a human begins and AI judgement ends. The ethical and legal quagmire that this could create in society could be enormous. As anyone applying for a bank loan nowadays will know, institutions are quick to hide their decisions behind a computer screen. So, in this instance, we should begin to be less worried about when the computer says no but perhaps when the computer says yes.

With AI expected to impact all of us in so many areas, it is no surprise that big businesses around the world are investing millions in research and development so that they can launch new AI-driven offerings. In fact, according to the research by CB Insights, the level of investment in AI start-ups this year is projected to surpass $10.8 billion (nearly double that in 2016). As part of the discussion around AI, the UK has an opportunity right now to attract this investment for our businesses and start-ups, perhaps creating the ideal environment here for a new AI-driven 'silicon valley' over the coming years.

If there is even a small chance that AI could impact our lives as some predict, then we must begin a serious political discussion now about how we want to adapt, adopt or legislate for its use.

I don't say this without some reference to history. When Tim Berners Lee invented the World Wide Web in 1989 and innocently sent his first message 'Hello World', no one could have honestly predicted how this would impact the world around us. Less than three decades on, the impact has been immense, both positively and negatively, from the decline of the high street to the rise of new businesses and careers, access to the world's information with a click of a button to the rise of global terrorism using social media to proliferate vile propaganda. On a more personal level for us all, the web is slowly changing our concept of privacy and what we allow (or unwittingly allow) others to know about us. Today, we face risks of hacking by people or governments, but imagine what hacking by an autonomous and unrelenting AI could mean for our privacy, security, and even our sense of identity.

Unlike the web, we may not have the luxury of time for AI to have a similar, unanticipated, impact on the world around us. Surely, we must plan for all likely (and unlikely) scenarios before we find we are playing catch-up. Even if there is a small chance AI could become smarter than us, then surely, we must work together to understand what this might mean for society, economic growth, the workplace, law, and even war.

Politically speaking, while I am no fan of quangos; due to the potentially far reaching impact of AI, this is one situation where I believe it makes sense to connect the dots across all of government, business and society through the creation of a watchdog or similar body to engage, understand, and set recommendations around the UK's approach to AI. Surely it makes sense to begin discussions now around how we, as a society, can apply the benefits of AI to the UK whilst exploring the risks of us all becoming unknowing slaves to the machine.

While the Roman poet Juvenal asked, "Quis custodiet ipsos custodies" (Who watches the watchmen), perhaps in this modern age we should be asking similar questions about AI, most notably (but not as elegantly), "Who will be intelligent enough to control artificial intelligence?"

Reviving Conservatism in the Capital

-- by Nabil Najjar, political consultant and director of Conservative Progress and former Conservative Party Regional Board Member and council candidate

The General Election in June did not yield the result that the Conservative Party was hoping for, but that is nothing to be surprised by. Coalitions and minority governments have masked the fact the Conservative Party has achieved a majority at just one of the last six General Elections, and has governed in majority for two of the last twenty years.

Yes, we are still the largest Party by both vote share and number of seats, but there are some facts that are inescapable, predominant among which is the fact that the Conservative Party has become unelectable in cities, and particularly in London. Demographic and cultural shifts mean that we cannot rely on our traditional base alone to win elections, and nowhere is this need highlighted more acutely than in London.

We lost seats such as Kensington that were previously thought to be unlosable, saw seats like Enfield Southgate and Battersea fall against the odds, and watched on as hefty majorities were decimated in safe seats such as Chingford and Woodford Green, Putney and Cities of London and Westminster and Chipping Barnet. Worse still, we saw Labour amass massive majorities in former target seats such as Hampstead and Kilburn, Westminster North and Hammersmith, negating the vast amounts of time and money spent there by the Conservatives over the past decade.

We cannot pretend that this was a one-off result, a Brexit-inspired, Corbyn-fuelled moment of temporary madness by the residents of one of the wealthiest cities in the world. In 2015, a Labour Party led by the inept Ed Miliband was able to gain a number of seats from the Conservatives across the capital, including Ealing Central and Acton, Ilford North and Enfield North. These losses were partially offset with gains against the Liberal Democrats in the South West, but many felt cause for concern, which was further compounded by Sadiq Khan's resounding victory against Zac Goldsmith in 2016.

We face some major challenges in the Capital in the coming years, with local elections next year and the chance to unseat Sadiq Khan in 2020. The harbingers of doom have already begun circling, decrying our prospects of a revival. I would not be so hasty in writing off the Party's chances of electoral progress in London, but need to rethink the way we campaign in London if we are to have any chance of being competitive in the coming years.

In this chapter, I will be outlining some of the changes we need to see if we are to mount a revival in the capital.

Policy

It is essential that we improve our campaigning machine, embrace digital means of communicating with voters and improve our community outreach, but none of that matters if what we have to say simply isn't worth listening to. It doesn't matter how good the salesman is, or how smart the sales tactics are – if the product is no good, people won't buy it.

The root cause of our electoral failings in 2017 was a failure to present a vision for how another five years of Conservative government would improve the lives of voters. Parliamentarians and candidates slavishly parroted prefabricated soundbites about Brexit, but when faced with Labour's platform of policies, we failed to counter with anything substantial of our own.

All voters, regardless of age, gender or race need a reason to vote Conservative, and in 2017 we simply failed to provide one. Our lacklustre campaign, sparsely populated policy platform and zealous focus on Brexit paled in comparison to Labour's optimistic vision for the future of London.

We failed to provide vision, hope or cause for optimism for the residents of a city in which life can be tough. Increasing costs of living, renting and home-ownership have priced Londoners of their own city. We failed to speak to the concerns of voters in the capital, neglected to present a policy platform that addresses these concerns, and paid the price for a lazy, one-size fits all general election campaign, which failed to consider the audience when crafting the message. It was absurd to campaign on a Brexit-centric platform in parts of London where 70% of people voted remain, to present no vision for young people in one of the youngest and most vibrant cities in the country, and to fail to present a path to home ownership in a city where both buyers and renters are being priced out.

We need to do better in London, and give the city the prominence it deserves in our policy making process, and the first step towards doing that is to acknowledge the place London holds in the hearts of the people who live and work within it. London is a multicultural, diverse and dynamic hub which draws in people from across the country and across the world. The city has itself become a unifier of its citizens. Being a Londoner is something people now identify with, and are proud to embrace, regardless of age, gender or profession.

The capital's residents face the same challenges – how do I survive and thrive in London. We need to present all Londoners with a plan for how we make that task easier.

To do that, we need to develop a separate set of London-specific policies which we can market effectively in the capital. We need to rethink the way we construct policy, and begin to consider the locality of the audience when presenting it.

We have a specific policy platform for Scotland, Wales, Northern Ireland and the North. It is time for a Manifesto for London, developed alongside Party members, Councillors, and the GLA Conservatives, which puts the priorities of Londoners at its heart – encouraging home ownership in every way possible, fostering entrepreneurship, improving public transport, cutting crime and embracing technology that improves the lives of residents. This will provide the intellectual ammunition we need to fight effectively on the ground.

Once we start developing substantive, targeted, well thought out and most importantly Conservative policies, focusing on these issues, then we will have developed a platform we can take into communities across the City. We can then begin to craft effective and local messages that resound at a local level, intertwining local issues within a city-wide framework.

Improving our campaign infrastructure

The Labour Party and their affiliated groups, such as Momentum, have us outnumbered in London, and they will be preparing to throw vast numbers of activists at target councils and target seats across the city. Seizing on a positive result at the General Election, Labour and Momentum have already started organising large-scale campaign days in seats such as Chingford and Woodford Green, and have begun running training camps to better equip activists to campaign on the ground.

If we cannot match them for numbers, we need to insure we campaign smarter. We will need to develop a localised infrastructure and campaign strategically to deliver our message at a targeted level. We need to develop a London-wide activist network to try and ensure resources are diverted to where they are needed. We need to invest in digital campaigning and social media skills development to compete effectively. We need to trust that local associations understand what messages will work best in their own constituencies, and empower them with the resources they need to deliver those messages.

Most importantly though, we need to reach out beyond our traditional base and increase our pool of potential voters. It is estimated that as many as 65% of BME voters cast their votes for Labour at the General Election, and it is reasonable to assume that, in London, that figure will be even higher. If we allow that trend to continue unchecked then we will never be competitive in London again.

It is vital if we are to be competitive in London going forwards that we embrace the opportunities and challenges posed by its ever-changing demographics.

Embracing digital

We need to invest in training for our candidates, activists and association officers and staff, ensuring proficiency in contemporary campaigning tools. For a fraction of the cost of delivering a leaflet across the constituency in the hope that it is glanced at on the way from the doormat to the bin, associations can develop and distribute digital content which will deliver more information to the viewer, incite a reaction, and allow the association to gather useful data in the process.

Developing an understanding of online campaigning is essential, and the Party has to help its activists harness the power of digital to win elections. Simply posting generic commentary and retweeting central office tweets is not enough. Effective use of social media and targeted online advertising and promotion are all essential tools in which all associations and candidates must be proficient. Understanding what campaign material is a good fit for each digital platform, and how target that effectively, helps generate a response from constituents.

Equally it is important that associations understand how their message should be targeted and delivered to ensure that it is heard by the right people. This involves using targeted ads and generating content that will be shared organically, and using understanding how to maximise the use of the 'backend' of social media platforms to better understand who is seeing, and reacting to, the content.

Finally, investing in professional-looking digital graphics and videos is essential to combat the stream of content released by the Labour Party and its affiliates, whether it is vox-pops, animations, infographics or candidate interviews, producing.

Selecting a champion for London as our Mayoral Candidate

People have already begun speculating about who our next Mayoral candidate will be, and common-sense dictates that the Party should select a candidate as soon as practicable to allow him or her sufficient time to build their brand, set out a policy platform and campaign effectively over a sustained period of time.

We need a candidate who is qualified and competent, but our candidate has to be much more than that. Sadiq Khan was such an effective candidate because he embodied what it means to be a Londoner. He was a man from humble beginnings who succeeded in a city which is open for business and welcoming to all. When juxtaposed against an uninspiring Conservative Mayoral campaign, it was a one-sided contest.

If we are to have any hope of challenging Khan in 2020 – and his weak record in office to date makes him eminently beatable – we need to select wisely.

Simply standing as the Conservative candidate and expecting to win is not going to work. The worst thing we can do is to select a candidate who is standing for the wrong reasons – expecting to lose and hoping to build their own brand within the party in the process.

We need a candidate who can transcend party political labels and reach out to everyone. That person will need to be the lightning rod for Conservatism in the capital, the mouthpiece through which new policies are announced, working with London's MPs, MEPs, Assembly Members and Councils to craft a unified, unifying message.

It could be someone from the world of politics, business or someone altogether outside the political bubble, but that person needs to be capable of presenting a real vision for a better city, able to inspire activists and voters alike. It has to be someone capable of being more than a politician.

Conclusions

The situation for the Party in London is problematic, but by no means is it unsalvageable. That said, we will not improve our electoral fortunes in the capital without first acknowledging the problem, and looking inward to better understand the reasons for this trend of poor electoral performance in London.

If we commit to moving with the times and developing the campaigning infrastructure that we so badly need, then we can start to see real progress. This starts with policy, and understanding the need for a specific set of policies for London, taking into account the challenges residents of this city face, and with home ownership at its heart. Only once this is in place can we begin to talk about campaigning effectively by establishing a separate London campaign structure, similar to that developed by the Scottish Conservatives and embracing contemporary, digital means of campaigning. Finally, we must select a candidate for Mayor with the energy and vision to reignite Conservatism in the capital.

The Future of the Conservative Party

-- by John Strafford, author of "Our Fight for Democracy" – a history of democracy in the United Kingdom

Introduction

Conservative Party membership throughout the United Kingdom was estimated at 3.1 million in 1951, falling to 1.5 million by 1975 at the time of the Houghton Report into the financing of political parties. It continued to fall and went down to between 350,000 and 450,000 by 1996, according to estimates compiled by Michael Pinto-Duschinsky, a leading authority on Party organisation and finance. After the 1998 reorganisation of the Party, membership picked up a little, but by nowhere near as much as the Tories hoped. The total had fallen to 320,000 by 2003. When David Cameron became Leader in 2005 membership was 258,239. By the time of the 2015 General Election membership had fallen to 134,000. In 290 Constituency Associations there were fewer than 100 members. Only two Associations had over 1,000 members and just fifty had more than 500 members.

In 1959 there were 500 Conservative Party Agents. By 1994 this had fallen to 200. Today there are fewer than 40. At a time when modern technologies such as computers have necessitated a more professional organisation, the need is greater than ever. This loss has been hard for the Conservative Party to bear. Agents take care of legal requirements, but more importantly they are motivators and organisers. At election time their loss could be disastrous.

Party organisation in many weaker constituencies is nonexistent. Some have effectively no Party organisation. Without radical change the Conservative Party as a Party of mass membership will cease to exist.

History of the Voluntary Party

To understand the reasons for the decline in Conservative Party membership we must go back to the origins of the voluntary Party.

The Reform Act 1867 brought an extra 1 million voters on to the electoral register. The new rules introduced by the Act and preparing for elections on the new boundaries ensured that an appeal to the electorate could not take place until the end of 1868. Disraeli's Conservative Party lost the General Election. It had spectacularly failed to learn the lesson of 1867 for they had not prepared adequately to face the new electorate that they themselves had brought into existence. Nevertheless, the passing of the Reform Act 1867, and even to an extent the anticipation that it would be passed led to the creation of more active Conservative groups in the boroughs and to the first organizations aimed at the newly enfranchised working men voters. Conservative Working Men's Clubs were encouraged and together with the local organizations created the National Union of Conservative Associations

The parliamentary leaders were anxious not to patronise working men's organizations too openly, lest they offend the middle class, at a time when middle class voters were rattled by the events of 1867 anyway. They were equally concerned not to allow too much room to these new Conservatives lest they ask for more. The remarkably deferential tones of those working men who actually attended the first conference of the National Union would have reassured them and there would indeed prove over time to be no great danger from the National Union, created (as the mover of the resolution that brought it into existence put it) not to rival the parliamentary leadership, but to be its "handmaid".[56] Until World War I all Presidents of the National Union were members of the House of Lords.

Disraeli created Conservative Central Office as his own private office. The three separate parts of the Conservative Party were thus brought into being – the parliamentary party, the voluntary party and the professional part of the Party, but they were not one body under one constitution. Each part was a separate entity. It was not until the Hague reforms of 1998 that a single body under one constitution came together.

In the 1880s Lord Randolph Churchill unsuccessfully called for the accountability of Conservative Central Office in the first attempt to create a democratic Conservative Party. Churchill wanted Conservative Central Office accountable to the Council of the National Union.

---

[56] Ramsden J., *An Appetite for Power*

When Lord Randolph Churchill emerged as the Leader of the movement for Party democracy in 1883 and 1884, Salisbury set his face against anything that he considered liable to fetter the complete independence of parliamentarians, as originally enunciated in Edmund Burke's 1774 address to the electors of Bristol. He was not about to allow parliamentary sovereignty to be circumscribed by caucuses of Party bureaucrats, let alone rank-and-file Party members. Control of Parties from outside parliament both seemed to Salisbury impractical, as it could not take into account the fast-moving mood swings of the Commons chamber, and repugnant in a Constitution in which an MP was expected to represent his whole constituency, not just that part of it which voted for him. There were therefore philosophical as well as practical considerations why Salisbury and Churchill were set upon a collision course.[57]

What Lord Randolph Churchill wanted was the transfer of all-executive power and financial control in the Party away from the nominees of the Leader of the Party to the Council of the National Union of Conservative Constituency Associations. In December 1883 Lord Randolph opened negotiations with Lord Salisbury, but Salisbury would not agree anything without assent from Northcote, who was the Leader of the Conservatives in the House of Commons. On the 1st February 1884 Lord Randolph Churchill became the Chairman of the National Union defeating Earl Percy by 17 votes to 15. This really put the cat amongst the pigeons. Salisbury communicated his displeasure through Percy, a Tory MP who later became the Duke of Northumberland.

On 6th March Salisbury and Northcote wrote to the National Union making it quite clear that the National Union was not going to be allowed to replace the Central Committee, which was *"appointed by us, and represents us: and we could not in any degree separate out our position from theirs"*.

Churchill replied the same day with the observation that: *"In a struggle between a public body and a close corporation, the latter, I am happy to say, in these days goes to the wall"*. A meeting of the Council on the 14th saw Percy suffering another defeat – this time by nineteen votes to fourteen – when he failed to reject the Organisation Committee's new definition of its own powers, even after reading out a letter from Salisbury opposing it".

---

[57] Roberts A. *Salisbury Victorian Titan*

Undeniably rattled by the course of events, Salisbury and Northcote then sent Churchill, via the principal Central Office agent, G.C.T. Bartley, an ultimatum, threatening to have the National Union ejected from Conservative Central Office altogether, "*to avoid any confusion of responsibility*". As the National Union had been faithfully paying its £175 per annum rent ever since 1872, Salisbury and Northcote were on doubtful ground legally, and relations merely worsened further.[58]

Bitter negotiations dragged on between Churchill and Salisbury until 2nd May when Churchill unexpectedly resigned as Chairman of the Council after losing a minor vote.

The 1884 NUCCA Conference opened on 23rd July in the Cutler's Hall in Sheffield, and resulted in an overwhelming personal victory for Churchill, who came top of the Council poll and Percy only eighth. As Churchill's majority on the Council had nonetheless fallen, there was room for a compromise, and at the Prince of Wales's garden party at Marlborough House on 26th July Salisbury and Churchill discussed the outlines of a peace deal.[59]

Agreement was reached. Whilst Salisbury gave way on several minor points the central concept was abandoned and even today the Leader of the Conservative Party wields enormous power by appointing nominees to vital positions. Why did Churchill give way? We will never know, but perhaps the unwritten promise of a future post in Salisbury's government proved a temptation too far.

Thus the first attempt to make the Conservative Party a democratic organisation failed, but other attempts followed. At the Conservative Party conference in 1905 members supported a demand for a democratic Party. Echoes of Randolph Churchill's attempt reverberated, but this was a more serious attempt to bring about change. Robert Blake noted: *"Joseph Chamberlain had a clear cut policy which everyone could understand; Churchill had not. Moreover, Chamberlain, from long experience of the Liberal caucus, was a past master at the art of mass organisation – a real*

---

[58] Ibid

[59] Ibid

professional; whereas Churchill for all his genius was a mere amateur at the game."

Balfour suggested the appointment of a committee. There were long delays before the committee was set up. While Chamberlain believed he could control a democratic Party. Balfour did not think that he personally could. In classic Conservative Party style, if you want to crush an idea set up a committee. This they had duly done and nothing was heard of it again.

There were early moves within the autonomous Constituency Associations to make themselves democratic. As they grew, the demands increased. With the increase in members the demand for representation in return for their subscriptions became more vocal.

The autonomy of Constituency Associations was both a weakness and strength. They kept their political independence, but sometimes to the cost of the National Party. In the 1910 General Election many seats went uncontested by the Conservatives because many Associations did not have enough money to fight an election, and although Central Office gave out a large sum in subsidies most of it went into hopeless seats and was wasted.

After the Representation of Peoples Act was passed in 1918 giving the vote to women aged over 30, the Conservative Party reacted by allocating a third of all positions in the Party to women. This stood them in good stead for after this they regularly obtained a majority of the women's vote.

During the 1920s the strength of the Conservative Party grew as it was realised that involvement and participation were the keys to success for the local Associations. Strenuous efforts were made to involve everyone. The result of this local democracy was a large increase in middle class members and in particular the women's organisation flourished.

In the 1930s most Constituency Associations had a Central Council and an Executive Committee on which the branches were represented. The Officers of the Association were elected by ballot and could only sit for a specified period. In some cases the Executive Committee, the most important body within an Association would meet on a Saturday so working people could attend.

The development of the Conservative Party organisation came to a screeching halt with the start of the Second World War. Mass participation became impossible and there was no appetite for political propaganda. Agents were dismissed; offices closed and as a result income in the constituencies dried up. Rich benefactors were as always notoriously unreliable. By the end of the War the Party organisation was in dire straits. In the General Election of 1945 it was to be tested and found wanting.

The end of World War II was a political watershed with the Conservative Party suffering what was then its then greatest electoral defeat. The desire for equality and a new era brought the Labour Party to power. The Conservative Party responded to the challenge by bringing in Lord Woolton as Party Chairman. Woolton was to serve nine years as Party Chairman and was probably the most successful Chairman in the history of the Conservative Party. He brought in the Maxwell Fyffe reforms, the most important of which were:

(a) To limit the amount of money a Member of Parliament could donate to a Constituency Association to £100.

(b) To recommend that Central Office should publish its accounts.

The recommendation to publish Central Office accounts was not implemented in full until 1993, some 45 years later. During that time the ordinary member could not force the Party to publish accounts because the Conservative Party had no legal existence. In a tax case in 1981 – Conservative and Unionist Central Office v. Burrell (H.M. Inspector of Taxes) – which was to determine whether Central Office should pay corporation tax or income tax on its investment income – it was decided that not only did it not have a legal existence, but it was not even an unincorporated association. The democratic power of the ordinary member was non-existent. You cannot easily change a body that is said not to exist.

With party membership at about 250,000 in 1945 Woolton realised that he had to build up membership in order to create, once again, a mass membership Party. He believed that one of the reasons for the defeat in the General Election had been that the Party had forgotten the "*little people*".

A membership campaign was launched in 1947 and by the summer of 1948, overall membership had increased by a million to 2,250,000, a spectacular success. The official (membership) campaign ended at the Party Conference in October 1948.

Woolton took on over 150 paid "missioners" who worked mainly in the marginals at Central Office's expense, and visited in 1948 over a million homes; at the peak in late 1949, there were 246 paid missioners covering 70,000 homes a week; their contracts were terminated for the 1950 campaign to conform to election law (though many were temporarily put on a different payroll as collectors of local political intelligence for Central Office).[60]

The *"missioners"* resumed work after the 1950 General Election but when the Conservatives were returned to government in 1951 the scheme was abandoned.

After another membership campaign in 1952, in which over 100 constituencies each raised over a 1,000 members, party membership rose to 2.8 million in England and Wales. If Northern Ireland and Scotland were included the total membership was a staggering 3.1 million people.

Participation was the key to this success. Swinton College was opened in 1947. Its role was to educate activists, train agents and volunteers and arrange lectures. The Conservative Political Centre encouraged local discussion groups and by 1947 there were 557 of them, meeting regularly in a member's house and all putting forward ideas and views on policy. The views were taken seriously by Central Office. It was part of the *quid pro quo* for the deference of Party members.

The young were not forgotten. In the summer of 1945 there were only 50 Young Conservative branches in the country. By 1946 this had increased to 1,546 nationally and by 1948 to 2,129 branches with no less than 150,000 members throughout the country.

---

[60] Ramsden J., *The Age of Churchill and Eden 1940-1957*

The figures for membership were staggering. In 1949 in Winston Churchill's own constituency of Woodford there were 12,898 members including 1,172 Young Conservatives. City areas were not neglected, with 60,000 members in Birmingham, two thirds of them women.

When Harold Macmillan resigned as Party Leader and Prime Minister in 1963 the National Union Executive was consulted on the change of Leader. This was a significant step for it was the first time that the voluntary Party had been involved in choosing a new Leader. In 1964 the process for choosing a Leader was changed. Hitherto *"the men in grey suits"* had done it with no formal process. The Leader emerged! Now, the Leader was to be elected by the Parliamentary Party - a step forward for democracy.

The political success of the Conservative Party during the 1950's and early 1960's led to reduced interest in making the Party more democratic but the defeat by the Labour Party in the General Election of 1964 brought attention to the lack of democracy in choosing the Leader of the Party. Edward Heath became the first Leader of the Party to be democratically elected by Conservative Members of Parliament.

The late 1960's and early 1970's saw the Young Conservatives at this time reported to have had 250,000 members try to bring democracy to the whole party by publishing a pamphlet called *"Set the Party free"*. It made a trenchant call for democracy at all levels of the Party including open selection of candidates and democratic control of the Standing Advisory Committee on Candidates. In spite of the support of Iain Macleod, the President of the Greater London YCs nothing came of these proposals.

In 1970 the National Union Executive Committee set up a committee chaired by Lord Chelmer to investigate *"the extent to which the Conservative Party in all its aspects outside Parliament might be made more democratic."* Chelmer's Committee had more than sixty meetings and produced a lengthy report. A motion, which called on the Executive Committee to prepare rules based on the principles of the Chelmer Report, was passed at the Central Council in 1973, but an amendment was also carried postponing action until after the General Election. The Central Council was the main forum of the National Union. It mainly comprised of Area and Constituency officers including the Women's organisation and the Young Conservatives. In this democratising mode minor changes were instituted. Balloted motions at

Party conference were allowed for the first time. Also Constituency Associations were instructed to use the same rules for the selection of parliamentary candidates, the first time indeed that any part of local procedures had been imposed on the Constituency Associations by the National Union as a condition of affiliation. After the Election the motion was quietly abandoned and nothing further happened.

The political success of the Conservative Party during the 1980's deflected any attempt at democratic reform. The Parliamentary Party began to believe that it did not need members and found it was convenient to ignore them. After all it was the members that held an MP to account. Without members there was no accountability. There was no national membership campaign until the "Bulldog" campaign at the end of the 1980s. By then the fall in membership was catastrophic.

In 1990 the party created Conservative Associations in Northern Ireland. For the first time the Conservative Party became a National Party representing all parts of the United Kingdom.

The General Election of 1987 was a turning point in terms of Conservative Party finance. Having finished the election with an overdraft, the Party embarked on an expensive refurbishment of Central Office and expenditure generally began to run out of control. By 1993 there was a £19 million accumulated deficit and a bank overdraft of £15 million.

In the two years to 1995 the deficit was reduced to £14.5 million. At 31st December 2015 it stood at £4.5 million.
In 1995 the Board of Management in its Financial Review referred to the fact that "the Party's Officers and Directors are satisfied that it is appropriate to produce the accounts on a going concern basis". Accounting rules were tightening and without this qualification it might be argued that the Party was bankrupt.

The Board of Management had been set up by Sir Norman Fowler (Party Chairman) after I published a paper in 1990 calling for such a Board. The idea was to bring all three parts of the Party together i.e. the Party in Parliament, the voluntary Party and Conservative Central Office. It was the first step in creating a Constitution for the Conservative Party.

In 1993, the Leader of the Party, John Major, asked me as an experienced campaigner for Conservative Party democracy to produce a paper on creating a Constitution for the Party. This paper was subsequently published by The Bow Group in 1994 and a campaign was started for the Party to have a democratic Constitution. The Bow Group paper was seen by Archie Norman MP who brought it to the attention of William Hague.

The Conservative Party suffered massive electoral defeat in the General Election of 1997. The new Leader William Hague immediately set in train a reorganisation of the Party. Initially he set out a vision of a democratic Party but by the time his proposals were finalised his vision had been watered down by vested interests. Primarily the Parliamentary Party was determined to retain and if possible increase its power. Initially the Parliamentary Party was only prepared to give the ordinary Party members 50% of the votes in a Leadership contest but in a speech at the 1997 Party Conference I demanded *"One Member One Vote"* this was then conceded. The Party at last got a constitution in 1998, but in accepting the changes the voluntary Party effectively gave up the autonomy of the Constituency Associations. They paid a heavy price.

Although the Conservative Party now has a constitution, that constitution cannot be changed without the agreement of an Electoral College consisting of members of Parliament on the one hand and the National Convention, which consists mainly of Constituency Chairmen, on the other. The real power resides with the Parliamentary Party. The Chairman and Treasurer of the Party are appointed by the Leader so are unaccountable to the membership. There is no Annual General Meeting of members so there is no formal forum for members to raise questions about the Party's organisation or policies. The Annual Accounts of the Party are not tabled for approval at an AGM. The Parliamentary candidates of the Party are controlled centrally. The Party Board can take control of any Constituency Association, which does not toe the line and has done so. When Slough wished to elect its own candidate for the 2005 General Election the Association was taken over by Central Office and effectively a candidate was imposed on them. Basically the Conservative Party is a self-perpetuating oligarchy.

The National Convention was set up by the 1998 reforms of the Party and is the senior body of the voluntary party. It was created to be the voice of the members and in its early days there were motions for debate and discussion of organisation. Gradually over the years it has changed and now it is a top down organisation with no debate or meaningful discussion. It has become a rubber stamp for the party hierarchy. It should be abolished.

Political Parties

Political parties play a major role in our democracy. At a General Election they issue a manifesto setting out their policies and use it to persuade the electorate to vote for them. The parties choose the candidates who will stand for election. From those candidates Members of Parliament are decided by the electorate. Members of Parliament from the Party capable of obtaining a majority in Parliament then form the Government, sometimes in conjunction with other parties - which have been through the same process - as happened in 2010, or sometimes alone.

The political parties choose their Leaders and one of them will become the Prime Minister. This is all very well if our political parties are democratic organisations open to all, but what if they are undemocratic organisations? Who exercises power in our political parties? Does it matter if they are oligarchies of the political elite? In such a case a small group of people will determine who governs our country and hence the policies by which we are governed.

Political parties are part of the democratic process in the United Kingdom. Their role is recognised by Parliament. In the current financial year nearly £7 million of public money, known as "Short" money, will be paid to the opposition political parties. During the period that the Conservative Party was in opposition, 1997-2010, it received over £40 million of public funding. In Government the gravy train does not stop. £8.4 million was paid in 2014 to the Conservatives and Liberal Democrats for 103 political special advisers. All this money is supposed to be given to enhance our democracy: it does no such thing. All it does is perpetuate the power of the oligarchs who run our parties. As long as the parties are able to rely on the State and/or big donors like businessmen or trade unions they can ignore their party members.

Both of our main political parties, Labour and Conservative, are undemocratic organisations run and controlled by oligarchies. Who are these oligarchs? They start with the Party Leaders, who are elected by the Party memberships. The Leader appoints the Front Bench. He or she exercises a great deal of patronage by creating Peers and giving out Honours. The oligarchs include businessmen who advise the Conservatives, and trade unionists who advise Labour. All are totally unaccountable to Party members. The net is spread wide. If the Parties had been successful in retaining the trust of the people, perhaps one could understand their desire to maintain the *status quo,* but the reality is that they are failed organisations whose membership has suffered long term catastrophic decline, and public confidence is in free fall. Soon, as membership organisations they will cease to exist. The recent increase in the Labour Party's membership since the General Election is due solely to its Leadership contests; these always bring an increase in membership because it is the one time when members know that their vote counts. In the two weeks after David Cameron resigned as Prime Minister the Conservatives gained 50,000 new members who believed they would have a vote in the leadership election. In the event no vote was held but at least the new members replaced the 40,000 members the Party lost in the first few months of 2016. A year later and many of those 50,000 have not renewed their membership fees and once again membership is plummeting to the 100,000 level.

Since the General Election of 2015 the Labour party has had two leadership elections and in the process gained some 400,000 new members and registered supporters. There are about 140,000 registered supporters who initially paid £3.00 to join, but of these 40,000 were deleted from the electorate for the 2016 leadership election for supporting other parties.

William Hague said that the Conservative Party was *"like an absolute monarchy moderated by regicide"* The Country abolished absolute monarchy and regicide 350 years ago. It is time for all parties to follow suit and examine the powers exercised by their party leaders. For too long they have behaved like absolute monarchs.

Candidates

Why cannot any registered member of the Conservative Party be a candidate, subject only to vetting to ensure that they have no criminal convictions and comply with electoral law? It should be up to the members of the Party to determine who shall be their candidate. This is a fundamental principle. If the members do not decide, who does and how are they accountable to the members?

The selection of parliamentary candidates of the Conservative Party is controlled centrally, by controlling the Approved List of candidates.

We have heard a lot recently about how the range of candidates should be widened and the Conservative Party have made much of Open Primaries. The model for Open Primaries is the United States so how do Conservative Open Primaries compare?

In the United States anyone can stand. In the Conservative Party the candidates are centrally sifted and three or four candidates put forward. In many States electors have to register support for the Party in order to vote. With the Conservatives anyone on the Electoral Roll can vote in an Open Postal Primary or an Open Meeting Primary, even if they are members of another Party.

The candidates in the United States raise their own funds for campaigning in the Primary. The problem with this is that candidates who win primaries are often those with most money to spend. "Pork Barrel" politics still has a big role to play in United States politics. The Conservative Party pays for a postal primary. The costs in Totnes amounted to £38,000. There are only half a dozen constituencies in the country that could afford this, so unless the Party at national level pays, or State Funding is given, postal Primaries will be few and far between.

Campaigns in the United States are usually prolonged, giving plenty of time to investigate the candidates. The campaigns run by the Conservatives are strictly limited in time.

Caucus meetings of registered voters are held in the United States at which the merits of the different candidates are debated and then voted upon. These are banned by the Conservative Party.

A distinction should be drawn between Open Primaries where there is a postal ballot as in Totnes and Open Meeting Primaries. The most common, because of costs are the Open Meeting Primaries. The Conservative Party imposes a number of restrictions on Open Meeting Primaries:

The meetings are advertised in the local paper so there is no guarantee that every elector is aware that the selection is taking place.

At the meeting no debate is allowed between the candidates – they are not even allowed to be on the platform together.

The elector must be present for the entire meeting and cannot leave the room for any reason. Contrast this with a postal primary where the elector doesn't have to hear any candidate before voting.

Limits are imposed by Central Office on the amount of money candidates can spend on their campaigns.

The vote on the final adoption of the selected candidate is by Conservative Party members.

It can be seen from the above that there are major differences between what the Conservatives call Open Primaries and what in practice most people understand as Open Primaries. The Conservative Open Primaries are a gimmick. The people and the media have been hoodwinked into believing that the process is open. It is not. The process is controlled in detail by the Party hierarchy. There is also the danger that the selection can be manipulated by the members of other parties, who can vote for the weakest candidate. The Conservative Party does not care, because it has decided on who the candidates will be.

Some Constituency Associations now run Open primaries for local government elections. In these cases, the sift of candidates is done by people accountable to the members of the particular Association, so the fundamental objections do not apply.

One of the objections to allowing the members to determine who their candidate shall be is that in many constituencies there are very few members and they may be unrepresentative of the voters. In the Conservative Party it is estimated that about 130+ Constituency Associations have virtually ceased to exist. In such circumstances it is reasonable for there to be a minimum number of members taking part in the selection process and where that minimum is not reached Party Headquarters has to take over the process.

In Hong Kong in 2014 the people took to the streets in protest at the Chinese Communist Party imposing a short list of four candidates for the people to choose from. Yet this is the very same process that is used by the Conservative Party in the United Kingdom.

Whenever Approved lists are used or procedures are implemented for the selection of candidates those taking the decisions should be democratically accountable to the ordinary Party members.

Membership

A major factor in the reduction in turnout at General Elections is the long term decline in the membership of our traditional three main political parties. Coinciding as it does with growing popular dissatisfaction with the political process, this has produced a toxic mix. Party activists represent approximately 10% of members and the decline in membership has led to a corresponding decline in activists. It is the activists who work to get the electorate out to vote. Critically it is feet on the ground that gets that last marginal voter to the polling station.

In 1950 when turnout at the General Election was 83.9% there were approximately 310,000 party members working to get out the Conservative vote. By the 2015 General Election when turnout was 66%, there were 13,400 members trying to do the same. Activist members of the Conservative Party are now primarily local Councillors and their families. After the elections of 2016 there were 8,496 Conservative Councillors in the United Kingdom

Individual Labour Party membership in 1951 was about 1 million. At the time of the 2015 General Election it was less than 200,000, so activist numbers had declined from 100,000 in 1951 to 20,000 by 2015. The Labour Party gets significant help from trade unionists but we have seen a decline in the membership of trade unions also, from some 12 million to 6.5 million. Some 70% of Labour MPs are linked with the trade unions.

So from a party activist base of a combined total for the two main parties of over 400,000 in 1950, it declined to 33,400 by the time of the 2015 General Election.

Why has this happened? What effect will it have and can anything be done to change this disastrous trend?

The number of people not properly registered to vote has risen substantially from 3.9 million in 2000 to 7.5 million in 2012 per the Electoral Commission. As at December 2015 the Electoral Register was only 84% complete meaning that over 7 million people were not registered. A major factor affecting voter registration is the decline in membership of the political parties. Political parties originated in their modern form as registration societies set up in the 1830s after the passing of the 1832 Reform Act. Their function was to ensure that all those entitled to vote were registered and did vote. Today this function has almost ceased, except in some marginal constituencies, because there are no longer the activists to do the work. Under the Reform Act only if a person's name was on the electoral register could he vote. Eligible voters had to register for a fee of one shilling (5p).

Let me expand on this point from my own experience. I was Chairman of the Gerrards Cross branch of the Beaconsfield Constituency Association from 1977 to 1980. Gerrards Cross was the largest Conservative branch in the country with a membership of over 2,000. It was one of some twenty branches in the Beaconsfield Association. The Beaconsfield Association today, in total, has about half the number of members of the Gerrards Cross branch in 1980, and yet it is one of the largest Constituency Associations in the country.

In 1980 Gerrards Cross had a committee of 38 people elected annually. It was a requirement of standing for the committee that you had to take on a road in the town where you would do the canvassing and collection of membership subscriptions. The membership was approximately 40% of the electorate. Each year when the Electoral Register was published one of the prime functions of the branch was to check that all members and all Conservative supporters were on the Register. A list of errors was sent to the Electoral Registration Officer so that the Register could be altered before the Register was finalised.

The result of all this work was that few people were left off the Register and the final Register was accurate. Branches of political parties throughout the country were doing the same as Gerrards Cross.

So what are the costs to society of low voter registration and turnout? Potentially the costs will be significant. There will come a point when the legitimacy of the elected government is questioned because of the low turnout. Democracy is a process by which you determine the will of the majority. If the gap between the views of the majority and those elected becomes too great the people may say "What can we do to change this?" The only solutions will be major electoral reform, reform of the political parties, or revolution. Time is running out.

Research from the 1990s on party membership published in the book "*True Blues*" showed two main reasons why people join political parties. The first reason was for social purposes. People like to be and feel more comfortable with others of a like mind. There is a tribal instinct.

The second reason is participation. This has to be meaningful participation i.e. they either vote on decisions to be taken or vote for the people taking the decisions. It is this latter motivation which has not been met by the two main political parties. Party members like to be led, but they also like to know that the Leader has listened to them before he or she takes a decision. Effectively large numbers of people join these parties each year wanting to participate. When they find that they have no voice they leave, usually after a couple of years. Only by adopting a radical approach will we break this cycle of decline. I set out below the measures that need to be taken. It is a check list to which all parties should adhere:

- Party constitutions should be capable of being amended or changed by the members of the Party at a General Meeting of the Party on the basis of one member, one vote given a majority in favour of amendment or change. Proxy voting should be allowed.
- There should be an Annual General Meeting of the Party to which all members are invited. (Note: this meeting should not always be held in the same location so as to prevent it being skewed in favour of members from a particular Region.)
- The Chairman should be responsible for the Party organisation.

- The Chairman and Treasurer should be elected by the members of the Party.
- The Chairman should present an Annual Report on the Party organisation at the Annual General Meeting of the Party for adoption by the members.
- The Treasurer should present the Annual Accounts to the Annual General Meeting for adoption by the members.
- The Chairman of the Committee on Candidates should be elected by the members of the Party and should present a report on candidate selection at the Annual General Meeting of the Party.
- The Chairman of any policy groups should be elected by the members and should present a report on their workings at the Annual General Meeting.
- Motions for debate on policy should be allowed at the Party's Conference and voted upon. If due to time constraints all motions submitted cannot be debated the members at the Conference should be able to choose at least three motions for debate. All motions duly proposed and seconded should be put on the Party's web site.
- Regional/Area/Constituency officers should be directly elected by the members of the Party.

The most important of these provisions is the ability to change the Party's constitution on the basis of One Member One Vote.

If we believe in democracy the fundamental requirement for political parties is:

"No political Party should be registered with the Electoral Commission unless it has a democratic constitution which can be changed at a General Meeting by a clear majority of its members on the basis of one member one vote."

By adopting the above, participation would be guaranteed for party members. Some parties already have some of the above provisions in their constitutions. The Conservative Party has none of them. The Labour Party is still dominated by the trade unions although the Labour Party constitution has been changed so that its Leader is elected on the basis of One Member

One Vote including registered supporters. Both Conservative and Labour operate electoral colleges which distort democracy by breaching the principle of One Person, One Vote of equal value.

With all the advantages to be gained from an increased membership why hasn't the Conservative Party adopted these proposals? After all, nearly every organisation has an Annual General Meeting at which elections take place and reports are adopted. The answer lies in the use of power, patronage and vested interests by those that get to the top and a determination not to give them up.

Having climbed the greasy pole and got into parliament, MPs are primarily accountable to their electorate at a General Election held every five years. Making them accountable to the Party members who selected them during the five years adds to their sense of insecurity. Having effective control of the Party's constitution enables them to put a barrier between the party members and the parliamentary party. The Party hierarchy are unaccountable except in a very limited way to their parliamentary colleagues.

Patronage is the second factor which comes into play. The Party whips control the backbenchers with promises of promotion, knighthoods, peerages, overseas trips etc. and patronage is extended to the voluntary party to keep them controlled. Party Treasurers, Chairman and President of the National Convention, Chairman of the Women's Organisation etc. more often than not end up with a peerage or an honour as long as their tenure of office has not had any problems.

The third factor at play is vested interest. It is easier to raise £20 million from 40 donors in large donations than it is to raise the same amount in £25.00 subscriptions. Subtle allocation of government contracts, access to the Prime Minister and other Cabinet Ministers, promises of a seat in the House of Lords, other honours are the tools of the trade in keeping the party organisation running smoothly.

It is said that the Party Chairman and the Treasurers have to work closely with the Party Leader and that is why they are appointed rather than elected, but these arguments apply to every organisation so why is the Conservative Party any different?

The problem with these old fashioned methods of control is that the public is now more aware of them and the clamour for change is getting louder.

Policies

Who determines policy? Of the two main political parties, policy in the Conservative Party is decided by the Leader and is constructed by a small coterie of people around him or her. In the 2014 European Parliament election the Leader of the Conservative MEPs only discovered what was in the manifesto on the day it was published! The Conservative Party no longer goes through the charade of pretending that the members of the Party have any say. There are no motions for debate at the Conservative Party Conference. The Conservative Policy Forum has little, if any, influence on policy. The Labour Party has the National Policy Forum and policy discussion papers. Its conference sets the "framework" of policy, but the days when it was the conference which decided policy are over. The National Policy Forum has severe limitations. Few members know who sits on it or what it talks about. There is very little reporting back to members or consultation with members before issues are debated.

With the development of the internet Party members could and should be much more involved in policy making. The priority of policies has to be left to the Party Leaders but in determining those priorities they should be aware of the strength of feelings of the membership.

2017 General Election

At the time the General Election was called on 18th April 2017 the press were forecasting a 200 seat majority. Opinion polls were showing the Conservative Party on 50%. The Party's biggest problem was complacency, and in the event incompetence became a major factor. The result of the election was disastrous for the Party. So what went wrong?

The Boundaries Commission proposals were not yet law, thus giving the Labour Party a twenty-seat advantage. The Election result showed that the Conservatives lost thirteen seats. If they had waited they would have had a majority!

The Labour Party had a financial war chest so couldn't be outspent by the Conservatives. It would appear that Labour spent their money more wisely. The Tories poured a million pounds into advertisements attacking Jeremy Corbyn on Facebook, whereas for a fraction of that money Labour persuaded their members to share positive messages about Labour. Negative campaigning harms not only the victims but also those perpetrating it.

It was clear that at some stage the opinion polls would move in Labour's favour and Labour would then claim momentum. Exactly that happened.

It was also clear that at some point there would be some bad news and the Conservatives would receive poor publicity. I didn't expect the bad news would come as a result of the launch of the Conservative manifesto. It was an appalling document with hardly any positive points in it, and the presentation was abysmal. Instead of saying Winter Fuel Allowance was to be mean tested why didn't it just say that it would be taxed in the same way the Old Age Pension is taxed. The poor would get it in full and the rich would lose some of it. That is fair. The case on Social Care went by default because instead of saying how much we had increased the amount people would be able to keep we did not include a cap on how much people would have to pay. A Free Vote on fox hunting was promised which we know a large number of people oppose. Why antagonise them by putting it in our manifesto? These stupid errors would not have occurred if there had been a wide involvement in drawing up the manifesto. In the past, the Cabinet, Back Benchers and even some members of the voluntary party have been involved. It is the wisdom of the crowd.

After the General Election was announced on the 18th April, two days later the following announcements were made by Conservative Central Office to parliamentary candidates:

"We will not be advertising seats, due to time constraints. Each Conservative-held seat and opposition-held Target seat that is selecting will

be given a shortlist of three candidates to put to a General Meeting of the Association. There will be consultation between the Candidates team and the Officers of the Association in drawing up the list.

"In the case of the remaining seats that are not targets, the Chairman of the Party and Chairman of the National Conservative Convention will be appointing candidates after consultation with local officers."

This was totally contrary to the rules for selecting candidates and was only pushed through using the clause in the Party's Constitution which gives the Party Board the power to do anything in the interests of the Conservative Party. This is a clear abuse of power and it was totally unnecessary. With seven weeks to the General Election due process could and should have happened. There was much complaint as the candidates list had been culled after the 2015 General Election and new candidates were barred. Effectively only candidates chosen when David Cameron was Leader were allowed to take part. This caused great resentment in a number of constituencies, which wanted a local candidate or a member of the European Parliament on their short list. It is not a very good idea to upset your volunteers at the start of an election campaign.

The campaign started as a very personal campaign with the emphasis on "Theresa May – strong and stable" and vicious personal attacks on Jeremy Corbyn. The electorate does not like personal attacks. I had an official communication from my MP, Dominic Grieve, which did not mention the Conservative Party once. If you are going to make the campaign personal, it was a mistake for Theresa May to refuse to debate with Jeremy Corbyn on television. This gave the impression of her being afraid, and highlighted the problem with a personal campaign. There was no hope in the Conservative manifesto: nothing for people to look forward to; no vision of the future. Yet Labour's manifesto contained a lot of hope and promises which the Conservatives failed effectively to counter-attack. Ours was the most miserable manifesto in my memory.

In the week before Election Day the Prime Minister visited Slough. I went to the meeting which was held in a large industrial unit which was "To Let". Only Party members were invited and about 400 turned up. We had to wait in the rain for half an hour to get into the building. The Party's coach turned up and drove into the building and became the back drop for the speeches.

The Prime Minister walked in with Boris Johnson. Boris took the platform and gave a five minute introduction to Theresa May, all written down and with no spontaneity. Then Theresa May gave a speech of about 10-15 minutes all about "strong and stable". No questions. They both then departed leaving me thinking "What was that all about?" Any Leader knows that on an occasion like this you wander round the crowd shaking hands, motivating the troops and giving them hope for the battle to come.

My constituency of Beaconsfield, one of the strongest constituencies in the country, was asked to help in Slough (a Labour held seat with a 7,000 majority) and Harrow West (a Labour held seat with a 2,000 majority). In 1979 I took 110 members from one branch of Beaconsfield to help in Watford. This election the whole constituency struggled to get 25 members to help in Harrow West.

After leafleting in my own constituency I decided to go to Slough to help there. When I was Constituency Chairman of Beaconsfield we paid for a full time Agent in Slough, gave other financial support, manned several committee rooms and polling stations on Election Day after carrying out a full canvas of the constituency. We won the seat in 1987 and in 1992. Unfortunately in 1997 Central Office wrote off Slough and we were sent elsewhere: big mistake! It has deteriorated ever since and now has less than 100 members.

I looked for the address of their committee room on their web site. It was not there. Eventually I got the address which was on a rundown industrial estate with hardly any parking. I arrived at approx. 6.30 pm and when I said I would bring the canvassing returns back to the office the two volunteers told me that it was about to close and the industrial estate locked its gates at 7pm. I arranged to return the canvass sheets the next day. The canvass sheets were provided by Central Office and included questions where you marked the answers out of ten; each elector had a sheet, and it would take at least ten minutes on each doorstep. This might be great if you have 500 helpers in a by-election, but it is totally impractical if you can number your helpers on one or at best two hands. I asked how much of the constituency had been canvassed and was told 20%. There was no way that canvassing would be completed by Election Day. Feeling concerned at this I asked where the committee room would be on Election Day. They did not know. I then asked if the polling stations were being manned on Election Day. They didn't know.

Next I asked if they had a list of helpers. No, they hadn't. Tearing my hair out I then asked who was in charge: I was told it was a woman from Central Office based in Southampton. We did our canvassing and returned the sheets the next day at 3.30pm. The office was locked so we pushed them through the letter box. The result in Slough was an increased Labour majority of 17,000. I gave up.

The day before the General Election I went to Harrow West arriving at 7pm. Once again the address was not on its web site. On arrival I was told that the Harrow West committee room was closed but they were sharing a building with Harrow East which was open, so I delivered leaflets for the Conservative MP Bob Blackman who got in with a majority of 2,000.

On Election Day I returned to Harrow West to help in knocking up. The knocking up sheet was excellent with lots of useful information, except it did not show the address of the polling station. To my surprise I came across several strong Labour supporters, and then I noticed that in some cases the last contact with them was in 2012! We not only were knocking up Conservatives but also Undecideds. The Labour majority went up from 2,000 to 13,000.

It seems all these constituencies were following Central Office instructions. I am afraid to say that the clever clots in CCO have never fought a General Election on the ground. The result was a disaster. On Election Day party members were being directed to constituencies such as Slough where there was no chance of us winning, whereas constituencies which we lost were starved of people. It is quite clear that Central Office did not have a clue as to what was happening. At the same time Labour was pouring supporters into constituencies boosted by its membership of 550,000 (which has now increased to 700,000 since the election.) Approximately one third of Labour canvassers had never canvassed before so were part of the huge increase in new members.

The Conservative Party fought the 2010 and the 2015 General Elections by targeting marginal seats. They had to because they did not have sufficient members on the ground to fight a National campaign. There are huge dangers in this. What and where are the marginal seats? Some "guess work" will always be required to decide where to put our resources but it is "guess work" and can, and indeed did, go horribly wrong.

Party organisation should be the responsibility of the Party Chairman. He or she should control the campaign. All consultants, special advisers etc. should report to the Chairman and he or she should be answerable to Party members at an Annual General Meeting. The Leader determines policy and priorities. He or she must take responsibility for the political aspects of the campaign.

Without radical change the Conservative Party will cease to exist as a membership organisation and if that happens, oblivion awaits the Party. The Leader of the Party has to take radical action to change the structures of the Party to ensure this debacle does not happen again, and if she doesn't then we will have to get a Leader who will!

Conclusions

In all my years as a member of the Conservative Party I have never known a General Election so badly organised and a manifesto so incompetently presented. This election was the final warning call to the Party: reform or die!

The most important factor in the next General Election will be *"feet on the ground"*. At the margin it is the canvassing and the knocking up that will count most, and for that you need volunteers and the most committed volunteers are members. Political parties will ignore this at their peril and unless our two main parties reform themselves into democratic organisations their decline will continue until they cease to exist.

What is becoming increasingly clear is that our two main political parties must embrace democracy, member involvement and participation and otherwise, like the dinosaurs, extinction will be their destination. The Labour Party must break its link with the trade unions other than as an affiliated organisation. Voting rights should be reserved solely for the membership. Within the next five years the Labour Party faces a great danger of implosion. It is vulnerable to attack from the newer parties which will target its seats

The Conservative Party must break its link with big donors who wield influence by being members of organisations such as the £50,000 club. There is still a danger of complacency in the Conservative Party which having just won the largest number of seats and the highest share of the vote in a General Election, has a belief that they can just carry on in the same old way and results will come right in the end. Nobody has taken responsibility for the shambles of the organisation. The party Chairman who is nominally in charge is still there. The Chairman of the national Convention who should have stood up for the rights of the voluntary Party is still there. There is no accountability. Lots of information was gathered during the campaign, but unless you can get hundreds of supporters into every seat on Election day there will inevitably not be enough people to get the vote out.

The Conservative Party can no longer fight a General Election campaign on the ground. Labour has shown that by giving hope to people, by promising to involve Party members in policy making, by promising to make Labour a more democratic Party it can build towards success. Can The Conservative Party do the same?

Printed in Great Britain
by Amazon